BALLPARKS

Major League Stadiums Past and Present

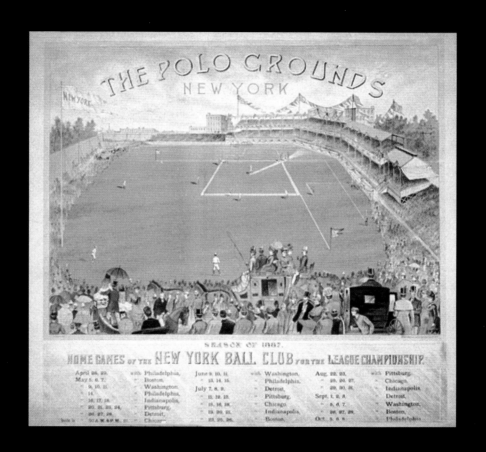

THE POLO GROUNDS
NEW YORK

SEASON OF 1887.

HOME GAMES OF THE NEW YORK BALL CLUB FOR THE LEAGUE CHAMPIONSHIP.

BALLPARKS

Major League Stadiums Past and Present

Robert von Goeben

BARNES
&NOBLE
BOOKS

NEW YORK

A BARNES & NOBLE BOOK

©2000, 2004 by Barnes & Noble Publishing, Inc.
Second edition 2004

ISBN 0-7607-5356-3

Digital imaging by Daniel J. Rutkowski.
Color separations by Bright Arts, Singapore.
Printed and bound in China by Midas Printing Ltd.

1 3 5 7 9 10 8 6 4 2

DEDICATION

To my wife, Kathryn, whose constant companionship at the ballpark brings me endless inspiration, as well as the latest gossip from *Vanity Fair*.

ACKNOWLEDGMENTS

Many thanks to Staci Slaughter and the crew at Pacific Bell Park. Tip of the ball cap to Doug McConnell and Jeff Magid, two of the squarest guys to come out of the windy city, as well as the Roach clan from the Big Apple.

Special thanks to the following teams for their assistance: Baltimore Orioles, Boston Red Sox, Chicago White Sox, Chicago Cubs, Cleveland Indians, Colorado Rockies, Arizona Diamondbacks, Seattle Mariners, Detroit Tigers, Houston Astros, Los Angeles Dodgers, Montreal Expos, New York Yankees, San Francisco Giants, Texas Rangers

Extra special thanks to Cory Suppes, whose incredible web site *Ballparks by Munsey & Suppes* (http://www.ballparks.com) is a must for any sports nut.

CONTENTS

Introduction: The Evolution of the Ballpark   **8**

Chapter 1: The Classic Era, 1900–60   **24**

Comiskey Park, Chicago (1910–90)   28

Polo Grounds, New York (1911–63)   32

Tiger Stadium, Detroit (1912–99)   36

Fenway Park, Boston (opened 1912)   40

Ebbets Field, Brooklyn (1913–57)   44

Wrigley Field, Chicago (opened 1914)   48

Yankee Stadium, New York (opened 1923)   52

Chapter 2: The Modern Era, 1960–90   **56**

Candlestick Park, San Francisco (1960–99)   60

Dodger Stadium, Los Angeles (opened 1962)   64

Astrodome, Houston (1965–99)   68

The "Concrete Doughnuts"   72

   Busch Stadium, St. Louis (opened 1966)   74

   Cinergy Field (Riverfront Stadium), Cincinnati (1970–2002)   76

   Three Rivers Stadium, Pittsburgh (1970–2000)   78

   Veterans Stadium, Philadelphia (1971–2003)   80

Olympic Stadium, Montreal (opened 1977)   82

Chapter 3: The Revival Era, 1990–present 86

Oriole Park at Camden Yards, Baltimore (opened 1992)   90

Jacobs Field, Cleveland (opened 1994)   94

Ballpark in Arlington, Arlington, Texas (opened 1994)   98

Coors Field, Denver (opened 1995)   102

Bank One Ballpark, Phoenix (opened 1998)   106

SAFECO Field, Seattle (opened 1999)   108

Minute Maid Park, Houston (opened 2000)   112

SBC Park, San Francisco (opened 2000)   116

Comerica Park, Detroit (opened 2000)   120

Miller Park, Milwaukee (opened 2001)   122

PNC Park, Pittsburgh (opened 2001)   126

Great American Ball Park, San Francisco (opened 2003)   128

Appendix: Selected Statistics of Major League Ballparks   132

Selected Bibliography   137

Index   141

The Evolution of the Ballpark

A fan walks into a baseball park on a bright Saturday afternoon. He hands over his ticket at the gate, already hearing the growing din of the crowd inside. Once through the turnstile, he tugs on his home-team cap and marches to the concession stands. The stalwart patiently waits his turn and barks, "A dog and a beer." With goods in hand, our hero turns the corner to get his first glimpse of "big green," the majestic spread of grass that is the thrill of any serious ball-field connoisseur.

As he takes his seat, he thinks to himself that there's nothing finer than baseball under the right conditions.

OPPOSITE: *Cubs fans mill around Chicago's Wrigley Field before the 1945 World Series against the Detroit Tigers.*

He checks the sky for rain, and surveys his view of the field. Good visibility to the action at first, and the scoreboard is in good viewing range. He settles in and begins filling in his scorecard. When the national anthem is belted out, he dutifully rises. All is as it should be.

Let's face it. Baseball is a fussy sport.

The lure and romance of a baseball park stems from a simple, undeniable fact: you can't just toss baseball players and fans into any situation and expect them to like it. More than any other sport, baseball is invariably dependent on the environment in which it's played. If it rains, the game's canceled. Snow? Forget it. Even a strong wind will make any hitter complain about robbed home runs, and shivering fans complain about the lack of "baseball conditions." Baseball parks come under relentless scrutiny. A great ballpark is a treasure to the community and a joy to be in. A lousy ballpark just stinks.

The genetic code for a baseball park was created in the early twentieth century, when many of the legendary American ball fields were built. From 1910 to 1930, many of the timeless features we associate with baseball parks (brick facades, grass fields, manual scoreboards) were first emblazoned in our subconscious. And like the smell of hot dogs and the bark of a stadium vendor, these striking sensations so unique to baseball have established a permanent place in our collective memories. From Wrigley Field in Chicago to Fenway Park in Boston, these early-century ballparks soon set the standard for sand-

lots that, before the century was over, would be established, lost, and rediscovered. By 1950 the definition of a baseball park was set: a small urban park that offered an intimate setting, a real grass playing surface, and grand entrances featuring turn-of-the-century brick architecture. There's no denying it—when a ballpark is right, you know it. Any fan surveying the ivy-covered walls of Wrigley Field in Chicago is sure to proclaim, "Now *this* is a ballpark!"

Baseball is unique in many respects, but none more than this: there are no rules governing the overall size of the playing field. This unpredictable quality separates baseball from its major league brethren: differences among the various fields are unheard-of in such professional sports as football, basketball, soccer, and hockey. All four are played on rectangular grids whose dimensions are strictly dictated. Imagine the Packers arriving in San Francisco only to find the playing field ten yards longer! This militaristic rigidity brings with it consistent stadiums, and for many fans it's tough to tell one field from another. And while the rules of baseball do dictate the dimensions of the infield, the outfield and foul territory boundaries are fair game, allowing ballpark architects to personalize each field, with unpredictable (and sometimes amusing) consequences.

Many say the best baseball stadiums are "quirky," yet lovers of the classic ballpark could never imagine why a home run fence would be the same distance in right field as it is in left—that would just be too boring. Fan preference notwithstanding, let us not forget that the blue-

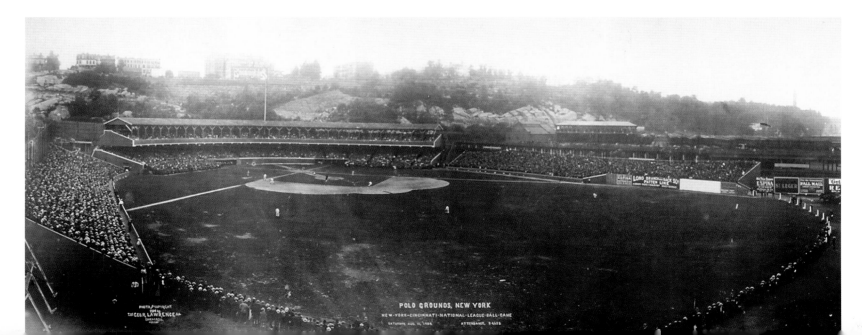

POLO GROUNDS, NEW YORK

Ballpark attire was much
more formal in 1911 than
today. Here, fans cheer on
the Yankees at New York's
Polo Grounds, a mere two
days before a fire destroyed
almost the entire stadium.

print for a lopsided stadium came not out of eclectic design but economic reality. Baseball owners simply took advantage of the loose field requirements to squeeze a ballpark into the small amount of land available in early-twentieth-century urban centers. Football came of age after World War II, and benefited from a plethora of suburban land; baseball grew up in a time when the game, like most of the population, fought for space in America's cities.

Furthermore, baseball is much more of a small-theater art than the "rectangular" sports. While a play in football can unfold over fifty yards, the key elements of a baseball game occur over inches. Baseball minutiae like balks require acute focus, the kind of attention that can only be appreciated when you're close to the field. Hell, you can pack a hundred thousand people into a football game; the referees are even piped into the public address system. But if you've ever tried to read the signs from a third base coach, you know that baseball requires close quarters.

By the late 1950s, baseball had grown up and was ready to expand. Existing clubs moved to greener pastures out West, and new expansion teams were added. Somewhere along the line the geniuses of baseball began to view the old ballparks not as treasured monuments but as old

relics. Not knowing what they had, postwar baseball owners rejected old ballparks for the suburban glitter (and potential profits) of monolithic "stadiums." Enter the modern era of baseball.

Baseball teams spent much of the 1960s and 1970s forsaking their historical homes and erecting gargantuan suburban monoliths, mistakenly thinking bigger parks meant bigger crowds. Like the teenager discarding his baseball-card collection, baseball owners rushed to the wrecking ball as park after classic park was bulldozed. First Ebbets Field in Brooklyn met the wrecking ball in 1960. A few years later, in 1964, Harlem's Polo Grounds met, coincidentally, with the very same wrecking ball. Forbes Field in Pittsburgh, Shibe Park in Philadelphia, Crosley Field in Cincinnati: gone, gone, gone. Hungry municipalities readily ponied up big cash in a quest for the biggest and best stadiums, desperate to avoid the brutal loss suffered by New York as both the Giants and the Dodgers packed up their bats and gloves and headed west.

The results speak for themselves. Baseball's classic parks were replaced by big concrete tombs, the best features of which were sterile symmetry and enormous capacities. These new monoliths were almost immediately hated by players and fans alike. Cinergy Field in Cincinnati, Three

Baltimore's cozy Camden Yards, which went up in 1992, marked the beginning of a modern-day ballpark renaissance.

ABOVE TOP: *The faithful watch from Coogan's Bluff as the Giants and Athletics battle in the 1905 World Series at the Polo Grounds in New York.* **ABOVE BOTTOM:** *Shibe Park in Philadelphia, opened in 1909 and demolished in 1976, was the first baseball stadium built entirely of steel and concrete.*

were satisfied, and the game's popularity plummeted. While the owners in luxury boxes may have lost touch with what made a great ballpark, the suffering fan never did. Try this some day: walk up to a fan in the stratospheric seats of Veterans Stadium in Philadelphia, look down at the glowing green of artificial turf, and ask him what a real baseball park is. Chances are he'll just look around and snort, "It ain't this."

By the time the century was coming to a close, the binge ended, and baseball teams woke up with large financial hangovers. Fans were universally rejecting the new breed of "concrete doughnut" stadiums. The era of baseball free agency had arrived, and invariably the teams that topped the standings were the teams that could get the butts in the seats, collect the cash, and lavish it on the pitcher with the 100–mph fastball, who was now commanding multiple millions per year.

The modern era officially ended in June 1989, when construction began on Camden Yards in Baltimore. The first baseball-only stadium to be built since Dodger Stadium in 1962, Camden Yards, with its brick architecture and downtown location, was a throwback to the parks of yesteryear. The strategy was simple: build a park that fans will enjoy, and they will flock there in droves. Next, use the increased revenue to buy better players; the team wins, more people come

Rivers Stadium in Pittsburgh, and Candlestick (later 3Com) Park in San Francisco were all designed with two things in mind: sharing the stadium with football teams and maximizing seat capacity. By the time stadiums had started ripping out the grass and putting in artificial turf in the '60s and '70s, ballparks had hit their nadir.

Come the 1980s, many aspects of the classic ballpark had gone by the wayside. Older baseball fans mourned the cozy confines of classic parks, and many younger fans grew up knowing nothing other than cold, sterile stadiums. Neither

to the stadium, and so on. Call it the ballpark formula for the new millenium; soon almost every team was trying to duplicate the recipe.

The turn of the twenty-first century will be remembered for a lot of things, but in the world of baseball there will be nothing more memorable than the slew of new heroes and old-fashioned ballparks. Just as Bonds, McGwire, and Ripken were ripping up the record books in the spirit of Maris, Ruth, and Gehrig, a new crop of retro ballparks brought us all back to the days of Ebbets Field and the Polo Grounds. From 1990 to 2003, no fewer than eighteen new major league stadiums went up in the United States. Paying penance for the past, many hope these new fields will revitalize the economics of baseball and at the same time instill a brand of civic pride denied by the stadiums of the '60s and '70s.

To be fair, this race for new confines also has its drawbacks. Baseball is currently suffering through an intense "have–have not" phase.

ABOVE: *Best known for its unusual rock formation in centerfield, Edison Field has been the home of the Anaheim Angels since 1966.*

A vendor hawks souvenirs to fans in the nosebleed seats at The Coliseum in Oakland, CA.

FAR LEFT: *Kauffman Stadium, home of the Kansas City Royals since 1973.* **LEFT:** *Warm-ups before the 1991 American League Championship Series at the Metrodome in Minneapolis, Minnesota.* **ABOVE:** *The hallowed halls of Yankee Stadium in New York, as seen from across the Harlem River.*

Granted, much of this inequity also has to do with television revenue. But when you're the Twins weighed down with the Metrodome, you understand that wanting a new ballpark is more than just "fussy," it's keeping up with the Joneses—or, for that matter, the Turners (the media mogul who owns the Braves). And never let it be said that a new ballpark is the solution to all ills. New confines are always a hit right off the bat, but it takes a winning field, as well as winners on the field, to fill the seats year after year. Just look at Detroit or Milwaukee, where lackluster teams led to a lack of keisters in the seats.

But for many fans, the business side is an afterthought compared to the experience of being in a great ballpark. From Jacobs Field in Cleveland to Coors Field in Denver to SBC Park in San Francisco, these new parks evoke a uniform but simple public sentiment: the ballpark is once again a great place to be.

San Diego's mammoth Qualcomm Stadium, which has a baseball capacity of more than 67,000.

With this, we return to the fussy fan at the ballpark. The last innings of an afternoon game play out as long shadows make their way across the field. He looks down at his scorecard, now stained with mustard, and relives the past couple hours of his life. Relishing the beauty of the baseball diamond and admiring the elegant simplicity of the steel grandstands, he realizes they were pretty good hours.

CHAPTER I

The Classic Era, 1900–1960

While ballparks quickly came of age in the first decade of the twentieth century, their humble beginnings bore little resemblance to the grand stadiums we know today. Baseball parks began as little more than fields, representative of the game's origins in the sport of cricket. In September 1845, a twenty-five-year-old shipping clerk named Alexander Cartwright formed the Knickerbocker Base Ball Club of New York, naming it after a volunteer fire company in which he had served. Cartwright began to fashion rules for a game based on cricket, but one that played much faster. On October 6, 1845, the first recorded game was played using Cartwright's new rules, which featured a diamond-shaped field. The historic

OPPOSITE: *Before it acquired its infamous color in 1947, Fenway's "Green Monster" was covered with a rainbow of advertisements.*

York Nine won handily, 23 to 1, and celebrated by feasting at the expense of the losers.

Baseball grew gradually from a clubby sport to organized contests, and eventually blossomed into a national obsession. By the first decade of the twentieth century, baseball had its National and American Leagues. In 1911 a new ball with a cork center was introduced, ending the so-called "dead ball era," and improving offense dramatically. As for the baseball diamond, it had progressed from fields to parks, then to stadiums. By 1909 it was obvious that the usual collection of wooden grandstands would not do. At the same time, improvements to construction techniques allowed for the building of more permanent structures.

The future of ballparks was sealed on April 12, 1909, when the magnificent Shibe Park opened in Philadelphia. The first ballpark constructed of concrete and steel, Shibe featured an opulent brick facade that became the trademark for many of the retro stadiums being built today. Shibe Park opened with an official capacity of 20,000, but more than 30,000 squeezed into the park on opening day, in keeping with early-century disregard for fire laws.

What started in Philadelphia soon created a ballpark frenzy across the United States. Between 1909 and 1923, new concrete-and-steel ballparks sprang up in Detroit, Boston, and Pittsburgh. Chicago got two new yards, and the greater New York City area saw the construction of a trio of classic halls: the Polo Grounds in Harlem, Ebbets Field in Brooklyn, and Yankee Stadium in the Bronx.

All of these classic parks had one thing in

ABOVE: *Elysian Fields in Hoboken, New Jersey, considered the cradle of American baseball, circa 1866.* **BELOW:** *Shibe Park in Philadelphia in 1910. A year earlier, over 30,000 excited fans crammed into the stadium for opening day, 10,000 more than its official capacity.*

game lasted a scant three innings, but in that short time, a national pastime was born.

By most accounts, the first ball field popped up in New Jersey, which is ironic since the Garden State has never had a major league team in the modern era. The upstart New York Knickerbockers sought a playing ground for their new game, and landed just across the Hudson River in Hoboken. The team settled in a green pasture known as Elysian Fields. Named after a happy otherworld for heroes favored by the gods in Greek mythology, the site was perfect not only for its floral beauty, but for the nearby taverns. On June 19, 1846, the first recognized baseball game took place as the Knickerbockers and the New York Nine slugged it out. The New

common: intimacy. While owners will inevitably want to cram as many people as possible into a ballpark, history has taught them that fans won't tolerate just any baseball environment. Throughout the twentieth century, ballparks took many different forms, from the casual fields of the 1800s to the 60,000–plus-capacity stadiums of the 1970s. But it was during this first decade of the 1900s that ball yards found their natural capacity, somewhere in the range of 40,000. For many intangible reasons, this

capacity just feels right, and it's no coincidence that most of the memorable ballparks of the twentieth century—Ebbets field, Wrigley Field, Camden Yards, Jacobs Field—had capacities in this range.

From the elimination of the dead ball to the introduction of the designated hitter, many different factors have shaped the game of baseball. But it was these oddly shaped, brick-faced parks of the early 1900s that forever forged the field of play, and our image of the game.

ABOVE: *Fans in "wildcat bleachers" enjoyed a free view of the 1914 World Series at Philadelphia's Shibe Park.*

Comiskey Park

Chicago (1910–90)

The original Comiskey Park in Chicago, with its successor waiting on the sidelines. The new Comiskey Park, now U.S. Cellular Field, replaced the original after the 1990 season.

Comiskey Park represented all that was industrial about Chicago's south side. Built in 1910 within spitting (and smelling) distance of Chicago's infamous slaughterhouses, Comiskey Park amounted to a no-frills workingman's ball yard. Born of humble blue-collar beginnings, Comiskey went on to have one of the most colorful histories of any American ballpark.

In 1910 owner Charles Comiskey found his White Sox doing pretty well, having bagged the pennant twice in the first decade of the century. Comiskey looked to move his team from their current home, a matchbox of a ball yard called South Side Park that held a scant 15,000 people, and brought in architect Zachary Taylor Davis (who later designed Wrigley Field) to design his new ballpark. But he also enlisted the help of White Sox spitballer and Hall of Famer Ed

Walsh, who helped design a decidedly large, pitcher-friendly park.

Comiskey Park was originally a double-decked grandstand that extended just beyond first and third bases, with single-deck stands extending to the foul poles and wooden bleachers in the outfield. Among its more proletarian features were view-blocking metal support beams, some directly in front of seats. The new park held 32,000 fans and cost $750,000 to build. Built on the site of a garbage dump, Comiskey was tossed up in just four and a half months, an amazing accomplishment considering the three- to four-year construction cycle of today's fields. In *Lost Ballparks*, author Lawrence S. Ritter recounts the story of how White Sox shortstop Luke Appling, smoothing the infield dirt before a game in the 1930s, met Comiskey's hasty construction foot- on. "I started digging with my spikes," Appling remembered, "and, lo and behold, I uncovered a blue-and-white teakettle. Quite an antique. The ground crew had to fill in the hole before play could continue."

Comiskey Park opened on July 1, 1910, and saw quite a bit of baseball history in the teens and twenties. In 1917–19 the park witnessed the World Series three years in a row, all of them quite memorable. In 1917 the White Sox prevailed four games to two over the New York Giants in what would be their only World Series victory in Comiskey Park. In 1918 the fall classic returned to Comiskey, but it was the Chicago Cubs who called the park home, losing to the Red Sox and the overwhelming play of a young Babe Ruth, his last year in Boston. In 1919 the Sox hosted and lost a World Series that they were accused of throwing.

ABOVE: *The slick new Comiskey Park, which opened in 1991.* **LEFT:** *Joe Jackson (far right) and other White Sox players in 1917, two years before the infamous "Black Sox" scandal.*

ABOVE TOP: *Baseball's first commissioner, Kennisaw Mountain Landis, throws out the first pitch at Comiskey Park on July 1, 1910.* **ABOVE BOTTOM:** *With some seats behind metal posts, Comiskey Park represented all that was industrial about Chicago's south side.* **RIGHT:** *Vintage White Sox beer coasters.*

When it was all over, Shoeless Joe Jackson and the infamous Black Sox had created a baseball controversy that lives on to this day.

Before the 1927 season Comiskey Park was substantially remodeled. The grandstands and the bleachers were double-decked, increasing the capacity to 52,000. At the same time, center field expanded to 440 feet (134m), further cementing Comiskey's reputation as the pitcher's best friend. Comiskey Park's massive scale intimidated all but one: Babe Ruth, who slugged the only ball ever hit out of Comiskey Park, in the fall of 1927. In 1934 home plate was moved 14 feet (4m) forward to give the newly acquired Sox slugger Al Simmons an advantage in the home run department. But Simmons turned out to be a paper tiger when the home runs didn't materialize, then a real Tiger when he was shipped off to Detroit in 1936. Home plate was moved back in 1937.

The White Sox had a long history of tinkering with their ballpark to achieve home-field advantage. In the late 1940s Sox general manager Frank Lane had the habit of moving the outfield fences depending on what team was visiting, leading the league to pass the "Lane Rule" limiting fence movements to one a year. But the most memorable field dabbling came from the ground crew. In the late '60s Comiskey's field was overseen by the infamous Bossard family, who to this day remain the recognized experts in groundskeeping. Among the numerous tricks employed by the Comiskey groundskeepers were cutting the grass long or short to assist Sox fielders, and raising and lowering the mound to upset visiting pitchers' rhythm.

In March 1959 the White Sox were bought by a syndicate headed by Bill "Voom Voom" Veeck, and the fun really began. He immediately painted the park white, and installed picnic tables within view of the park. But his most outlandish renovation was the addition of baseball's first exploding scoreboard in 1960. Costing $30,000, Veeck's technological wonder stood 130 feet (40m) tall in center field and was designed to blow its top every time a White Sox player hit a home run. Nicknamed the Monster, the scoreboard unleashed a thirty-two-second cacophony of sirens, horns, and fireworks, all to the tune of the *William Tell* Overture. Fans went wild, though visiting teams were not impressed; Detroit manager Jimmy Dykes was known to have whined, "What is this, Disneyland?" But the last word on the Monster came from Casey Stengel's Yankees, who stood in front of the bullpen waving sparklers when Yankee third baseman Clete Boyer hit one over the fence in 1960.

Due to failing health, Veeck sold the club in 1961 and moved to the East Coast, but by 1975 Veeck was back in the pink. He reacquired the White Sox, and the wild promotions continued. None topped the now-infamous "Disco Demolition Night" held at Comiskey Park on July 12, 1979. Fans were encouraged to bring their disco records to the stadium, which were to be burned between games of a doubleheader against the Detroit Tigers. More than 47,000 attended, but the sight of thousands of disco records burning in center field proved too much for the fans, who rioted and stormed the field, causing the White Sox to forfeit the nightcap to the Tigers.

Veeck sold the White Sox in 1981 to a syndicate of Chicago businessmen led by Jerry Reinsdorf. The new owners looked into renovating Comiskey but ultimately deemed Comiskey too old and outdated, and threatened to move the team if a new stadium wasn't built. With communities in Florida and Wisconsin attempt-

ing to lure the White Sox with promises of fancy new stadiums, the Illinois Legislature designated funds for a new Comiskey Park to be built across the street from the old one. The last game at the old Comiskey Park was played on September 30, 1990, against the Seattle Mariners.

To this day old Comiskey Park still holds a place in the hearts of many White Sox fans. While many agree that the old park had seen better days, critics say that although the new Chicago White Sox ballpark provides more amenities, it lacks the character of the old yard. Some describe the new Comiskey Park, which opened in 1991 and was renamed U.S. Cellular Field in 2003, as a cold and impersonal place whose steep upper decks serve only the interests

of luxury-box revenue. But even the staunchest admirers admit it was time for the old Comiskey to hit the showers. Chicago native and lifelong Sox fan Jeff Magid remembers visiting the old Comiskey shortly before its closing:

Looking around Comiskey with the realization that it would be demolished, I recalled the exciting games I'd seen in my youth. I duly noted all the metal posts I sat behind. Then awash in memories as I left the stadium, my thoughts were simply this: WHAT A DUMP THIS BALLPARK IS! IT HAS ALL THE CHARM OF A STEEL MILL! GOOD RIDDANCE!

Some say U.S. Cellular Field, with its ultra-steep upper deck, lacks the charm and intimacy of its predecessor.

ABOVE: *A program from the 1912 World Series. The Giants' stadium was originally called Brush Stadium, a name that never stuck.* BELOW: *An 1887 printed schedule for The Polo Grounds, the first of three New York ballparks to carry that name.*

Polo Grounds

New York (1911–63)

The home of the New York Giants for forty-six years, the Polo Grounds was a hallowed hall of baseball history. As one of the famous troika of New York ballparks that also included Yankee Stadium and Ebbets Field, the Polo Grounds was home to not one but three major league teams. Besides the Giants, both the Yankees and the Mets called the Polo Grounds home at one time or another.

Irrespective of the field's name, polo was never played at the Polo Grounds. The longtime home of the New York Giants was in fact the fourth park to carry the name. In 1883 John B. Day brought his independent team, the Metropolitans, from Brooklyn to a former polo sight near Central Park after getting a tip on the site from a shoe-shine boy. Day's team played at this original Polo Grounds for five years, until they were evicted by the city of New York after the 1888 season.

For the 1889 season Day moved his team to a spot just under Coogan's Bluff, between 155th and 159th streets. In fact, there were two ballparks in Coogan's Bluff: the Giants brought the name "Polo Grounds" to the southern half, while the upstart Players League occupied the north-ern half of the meadow in a yard they called Brotherhood Park. The two parks were located so close to each other that home runs in one park would land in the other, causing the fans from both parks to cheer! But by the 1891 season the Players League had gone belly-up, and the National League took over the northern part of the meadow, bringing the Polo Grounds moniker with them.

This third Polo Grounds consisted of little more than a double-decked wooden grandstand, with bleachers in the outfield. The park held 16,000, including a spot in center field for well-heeled patrons to park their carriages. But this Polo Grounds was short-lived as well—the park burned to the ground on April 14, 1911. Less than three months later the Polo Grounds rose again, with temporary stands. By the time the Philadelphia Athletics rolled into town for the 1911 World Series, the Polo Grounds sported steel-and-concrete grandstands, and a capacity of more than 30,000.

The Polo Grounds inherited another tenant when the Yankees moved in for the 1913 season and stayed ten years. When the Giants met the Yankees in back-to-back World Series in 1922 and 1923, every game of the fall classic was played at the Polo Grounds. Relative harmony between the two teams existed for six years

until 1919, when the Yankees acquired Babe Ruth from the Red Sox. Ruth cherished the short fences of the Polo Grounds, and his frequent home runs were making the Yankees the darlings of the box office. This success thrilled fans but irked John McGraw, the fiercely competitive owner of the Giants. The Yankees were booted from the Polo Grounds in 1922, and in 1923 took up residence in Yankee Stadium, their new palace located just across the Harlem River in the Bronx. But the exit was not without some regret on the part of Ruth, who had done so well at the Polo Grounds. "Boy, how I used to sock 'em in there," Ruth lamented. "I cried when they took me out of the Polo Grounds."

Looking at the unique dimensions of the Polo Grounds, one can understand Ruth's love for the park. The stadium was modeled in a bathtub shape, which allowed for incredibly short distances at the foul poles—279 feet (85m) in left field and 257 feet (78m) in right. And if that wasn't enough to make hitters salivate, the Polo Grounds featured a second-deck overhang in left field that extended beyond the bottom deck, making the home run distance to the upper deck a mere 258 feet (79m) in left.

Center field and the power alleys at the Polo Grounds were perilously long. From an aerial view of the park, the most obvious feature of

the submarine-shaped sandlot was the endless expanse of green outfield. The center field wall was 483 feet (147m) from home plate for most of the park's life, an insurmountable distance by any standard. It has been argued that one of the most famous plays in baseball history, Willie Mays's backhanded catch of a Vic Wertz fly ball in the 1954 World Series, never could

BELOW: *Bleachers at the Polo Grounds.*
BOTTOM: *New York's Polo Grounds in 1910. Six months later, a devastating fire would consume the ball yard, leaving only the bleachers standing.*

RIGHT: *Fire ravages the Polo Grounds on April 14, 1911. Little more than half of the seats survived the blaze.*

BELOW: *The Polo Grounds centerfield, shown in 1954, was challenging in terms of its depth, but with both foul poles under 300 feet (91m), the park delighted pull hitters like Babe Ruth.*

occurred in most other parks, where such a smash would have easily been a home run.

The Giants played decades of glorious baseball in the Polo Grounds, but by the late 1950s the sport was changing. The riches of California were beckoning, and the Giants' days in the Polo Grounds were numbered. With sagging attendance, owner Horace Stoneham announced in 1957 that the team was vacating Harlem for San Francisco. "We're sorry to disappoint the kids of New York," Stoneham is quoted as saying in *Baseball: An Illustrated History*, "but we didn't see many of their parents out there at the Polo Grounds in recent years."

For Giants fans, the impossible became reality on September 29, 1957, when the Giants played their last game in the Polo Grounds, los-

ing to the Pirates 9–1. Only 11,606 fans bothered to show up, some in center field waving a large banner that read "Stay Team, Stay."

Five years later the Polo Grounds was open for baseball again, if only temporarily. The newly minted New York Mets called the Polo Grounds home for two years while Shea Stadium was going up in Flushing, Queens. The fledgling ball club pumped $250,000 into the Polo Grounds to bring it up to speed. But after the Mets spent two years setting new records for losing (they gave up 120 games in 1962), the Polo Grounds were empty again. The old yard was demolished on April 10, 1964, devastated by the same wrecking ball that had razed Ebbets Field just a few years earlier.

BELOW: *The New York Mets moved to the cavernous Shea Stadium after they spent their first two seasons (1962 and 1963) in the far more intimate Polo Grounds.*

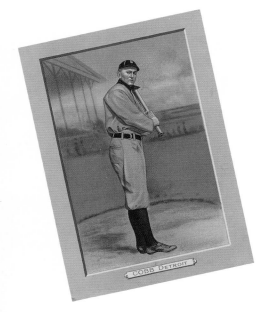

COBB DETROIT

Tiger Stadium
Detroit (1912–99)

Baseball today is caught in a tug-of-war between the past and the present, and the game struggles to retain its glorious history while keeping up with the economic realities of the present. No major league ballpark in the United States symbolized this battle of old versus new more than Detroit's Tiger Stadium. Before the battle was over, Tiger Stadium would sit at the middle of a unique owner-fan struggle that ended up in the Michigan Supreme Court.

Located for almost nine decades at the historic corner of Michigan and Trumbull Avenues in Detroit, Tiger Stadium has one of the most colorful and controversial histories in baseball. In 1895 George Vanderbeck looked to convert a Detroit hay market into a park for his Detroit Western League team. Bennett Park, named after a Detroit player who'd lost both his legs in a train accident, was little more than a wooden grandstand holding fewer than 10,000 fans when it went up in 1896. The modest park saw a tremendous amount of baseball, including the debut of the great Ty Cobb and three straight American League pennants (which led to three straight World Series losses) from 1907 to 1909.

By 1911 the Tigers were so popular that a bigger stadium was required, and new owner Frank Navin shelled out $300,000 for a new baseball palace that would hold 23,000 fans on the same location. Opening day for the new Navin Field, as it was originally called, was delayed two days because of rain, but the new park opened on April 20, 1912 (coincidentally, the same day that Fenway Park opened). Upon opening, Navin Field was little more than concrete-and-steel grandstands that extended beyond the bases, with small bleachers in right field. To the excitement—and benefit—of team owners, the new stadium required the demolition of a row of houses located behind the old left field, eliminating a series of rooftop "wildcat bleachers" that had been erected by bootleg fans.

The stadium saw a number of renovations, the first of which occurred in 1924. A second deck was added to the grandstands, which increased capacity to 30,000. In 1935, the year the Tigers took the World Series, new owner Walter Briggs looked to enlarge the stadium but, as Michael Gershman describes in *Diamonds: The Evolution of the Ballpark*, he ran into a problem expanding amidst tight urban confines. "Trumbull Avenue ran right behind it," Gershman wrote, "and there was no way to expand backward. Another problem was that Briggs didn't want to cheapen the home run by moving the wall in any way closer than 325 feet [99m]. Right field was shortened from 367 to 325 feet [112 to 99m], but to compensate, he extended the upper deck 10 feet [3m] beyond the lower deck in front and in back." The result was a "porch" hanging over the field onto which cunning hitters could bloop home runs. The home run porch became an indelible symbol of this old ball yard, and was the inspiration for a similar design at the Ballpark in Arlington, home of the Texas Rangers.

By 1938, the stadium (now called Briggs Stadium after its new owner) had undergone more expansion and reached a capacity of

58,000. Little change occurred in the new stadium in the succeeding years, except for the addition of lights in 1948 (the last American League Park to do so) and a name change to Tiger Stadium in 1961. While new ballparks habitually pulled in home run fences to increase long-ball action, Tiger Stadium's center field continued to stand at 440 feet (134m), one of the longest in the majors.

By the 1960s, with new multipurpose cathedrals popping up all over the country, Detroit remained faithful to its historic park. Writer Michael Gershman comments on Detroit's ironic pride in their ballpark, writing, "Such an attitude would be noteworthy anywhere in the United States; it is doubly so in Detroit, America's capital of planned obsolescence, a city whose civic leaders think not in generations or decades but in model years."

The fans at Tiger Stadium saw their Detroit team win three more Series, the first two in 1945 and 1968. But it was the 1984 World Series that made headlines for more than the play on the field. In the fifth and deciding game of the series, Kirk Gibson popped two out of the park to take the World Series from the San Diego Padres, and the Detroit faithful celebrated by going nuts. Fans stormed onto the field and destroyed the turf, and a riot broke out on the street. In the end, the fiasco ignited more than the cars that burned outside the stadium: the 1984 World Series riot heightened the debate over whether Tiger Stadium was ready for replacement.

Through the 1980s and 1990s Tiger owners and supporters went back and forth over whether Tiger Stadium should be bulldozed or renovated. Detractors questioned the stadium's structural integrity, as well as the safety of the surrounding neighborhood, while supporters argued that owners were more interested in profits and luxury boxes than in history. Manager Sparky Anderson, who led the team to the 1984 World Series victory, weighed in by saying, "Those who want to preserve Tiger Stadium and keep it for their grandchildren have lost their marbles." However, preservationists proved to be crazy like foxes, and well organized. In 1987 fans united against the new ballpark formed the Tiger Stadium Fan Club, a group that turned out to be a formidable adversary in the fight for the future of the old park.

The Tiger Stadium Fan Club and the team owners continued to argue over the fate of Tiger Stadium for years. In 1988, the fan club pulled a coup by getting Tiger Stadium placed on the National Register of Historic Places. This was significant because it meant that no federal funds could be used to tear down Tiger Stadium and build a replacement on the site. But the boldest move

BELOW: *The Detroit Tigers featured on a Fatima tobacco card in 1913. It would be their second season in Tiger Stadium, then known as Navin Field.* **BOTTOM:** *The 1909 World Series at Bennett Park, which stood for only fifteen years before it was replaced by Tiger Stadium in 1912.*

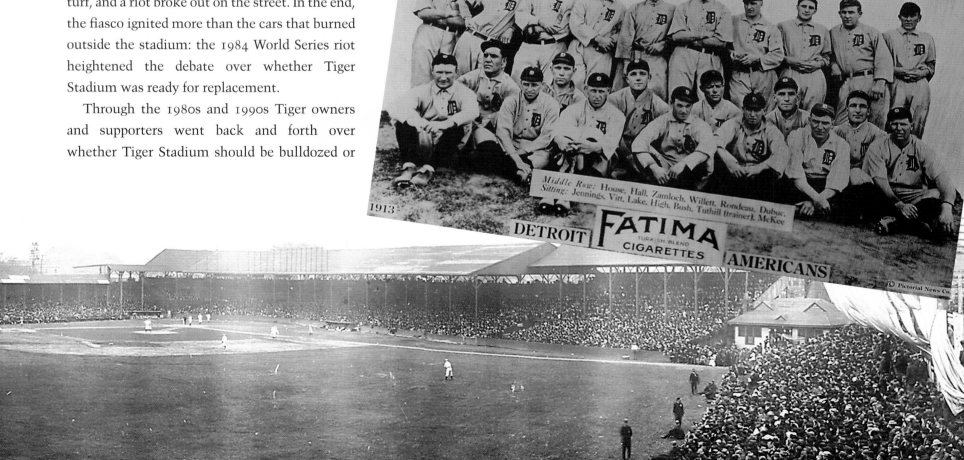

ABOVE: *An overhead view of the original Tiger Stadium in Detroit. Originally opened in 1912, the ballpark closed its turnstiles for good at the end of the 1999 season.*

RIGHT: *Historic Tiger Stadium, with its infamous right field "porch."*

came in January 1990, as the Tiger Stadium Fan Club made the unprecedented move of releasing its own plan for the preservation of Tiger Stadium. Dubbed the Cochrane Plan, after the name of an adjoining street, the plan was a Magna Carta for ballpark preservationists.

Nevertheless, Tiger owners, along with city and state officials, continued to pursue a new stadium. Even an $8 million renovation to Tiger Stadium in 1993 (which included a new scoreboard and other amenities) didn't stop the new-stadium tidal wave. In 1995 the Tiger Stadium Fan Club initiated a lawsuit challenging the funding for a proposed new ballpark. This unprecedented fan rebellion went all the way to the Michigan Supreme Court, which ruled against the lawsuit on July 17, 1996. In the end, with a court victory and money in their pocket, Tiger owners broke ground for a new ballpark on October 27, 1997.

The Tigers' new ballpark debuted on opening day 2000 and, in a sign of the times, is called

Comerica Park after the financial services company that paid millions for the naming rights. The new park is everything the rule book says it should be: with no upper-deck seats in the outfield, Comerica Park features a stunning view of the Detroit skyline. A cozy sandlot holding 42,000, the new Tiger yard has a classic brick

facade and a massive entrance with two 60–foot (18m) baseball bats and a massive Tiger statue guarding the entrance.

For the city of Detroit, the end of professional baseball at Tiger Stadium was the end of a long and emotional struggle that wrote an important chapter in the history of American ballparks.

As teams struggle to find new sources of revenue in order to compete for players, the faithful continue to debate the future of the game's ancient ballparks. And nowhere has this clash been more obvious than in Detroit. For better or for worse, Major League Baseball no longer calls the corner of Michigan and Trumbull home.

Fenway Park
Boston (opened 1912)

For the Boston baseball fanatic, there is nothing like the frenzied activity in front of Fenway Park prior to a Red Sox game. Fans dash in and out of cafes while the adjoining Yawkey Way swarms with vendors. Walking the perimeter of Fenway Park, the home of the Red Sox for almost nine decades, you can't help but feel the electricity of Boston and the city's love of its ballpark.

Bostonians have been experiencing Fenway's unique baseball magic since the park opened on April 20, 1912, the same day as Detroit's Tiger Stadium. And with the demise of the Motor City ballpark after the 1999 season, Fenway now stands as the oldest major league park in commission, a standard-bearer whose beauty and history have cast a spell over purists and reformers alike.

From 1901–1911, the Boston Pilgrims—predecessors to the Red Sox—played ball at the Huntington Avenue Grounds, which today is part of Northeastern University in Boston. In 1904, *Boston Globe* owner General Charles Taylor bought the Red Sox for his son John, and the younger Taylor immediately made plans for a new ballpark to be located in a swampy part of Boston known as the fens. The area had been drained a few years earlier when Frederick Law Olmsted, who designed New York's Central Park, planned a ring of parks

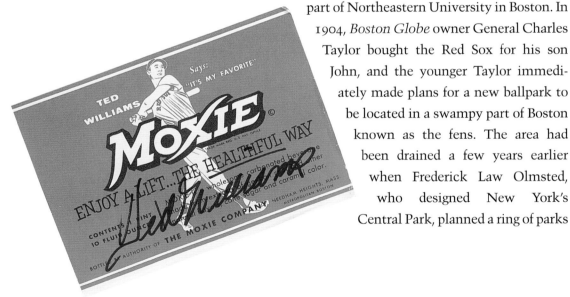

surrounding Boston. By the time the Red Sox were ready for their new park, the fens became an ideal location, mainly because the senior Taylor was a substantial shareholder in the Fenway Realty Company, which owned the land.

Together with Forbes Field in Pittsburgh and Shibe Park in Philadelphia (both of which opened in 1909), Fenway was one of a new generation of concrete-and-steel ballparks. Opening day saw Boston mayor John "Honey Fitz" Fitzgerald (grandfather of John F. Kennedy) throw out the first pitch at a ballpark that was quite different from the Fenway Park we know today. The original Fenway had a massive center field measuring 488 feet (149m)—almost 50 feet (15m) longer than it is now. Wooden bleachers and grandstands sat in the outfield. But the real story was in left field. Long before Fenway had a massive green wall as its trademark, left field was known for the 10-foot (3m) embankment that led up to the fence. So treacherous was this incline that it became known as Duffy's Cliff in honor of Red Sox left fielder Duffy Lewis, one of the few players who mastered the slope.

Shallow-pocketed owners prevented any major renovations to Fenway for the next two decades; even after a fire on May 8, 1926, owner Bob Quinn did nothing more than haul off the burnt remains of the left-field bleachers. But Fenway received a large cash infusion before the 1934 season, when new owner Tom Yawkey bought the team. Duffy's Cliff was leveled, and

wooden bleachers were replaced with concrete grandstands in right field. The most enduring improvement made in 1934 was the addition of a 37-foot (11.3m) fence erected in left field, a Fenway landmark that remains to this day. Constructed of 18 feet (5.5m) of concrete topped by 19 feet (5.8m) of wooden railroad ties covered with tin, the wall that would someday become known as the Monster was originally littered with advertising.

A ladder was attached in 1936 so that batting practice home runs could be shagged, and to this day remains the only "in play" ladder in the majors. Starting at just over 13 feet (4m) and going to the top of the wall, the Fenway ladder is considered a charming feature by most, except Sox great Ted Williams, who once watched a fly ball hit by Jim Lemon careen off the ladder and into center field for an in-the-park home run.

In 1947 Fenway underwent another renovation and the wall got its infamous coat of green paint, becoming the Green Monster we know today. This great wall of baseball has challenged a series of Red Sox fielders, from Ted Williams to Carl Yastrzemski. By 1975 the tin of the Green Monster had seen better days, and the wall was replaced with a hard plastic surface.

Nothing is more identified with Fenway Park than that intimidating, towering left-field fence. Loved by pitchers, feared by hitters, and revered by baseball writers, the Green Monster is one of the most endearing (and enduring) symbols of

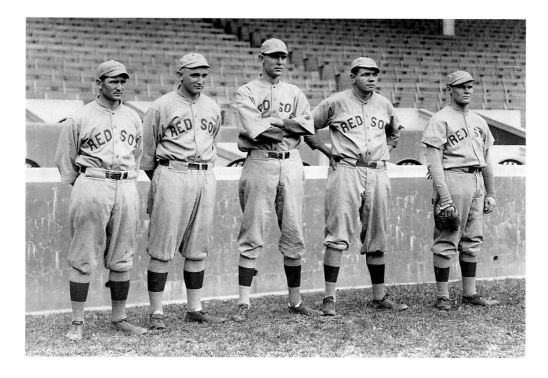

ballpark uniqueness. While many parks have built tall outfield fences, none has the mystique and allure of Fenway's Green Monster.

In April 2003, the Sox took the allure of the Monster even further with the debut of a small section of seats located directly on top of the Green Monster. These primo seats sit 310 feet (94.5m) from home plate and over 40 feet (1.2m) off the ground.

Fenway Park is one of the grand old parks of the game—as well as the smallest. Unfortunately,

with its outdated facilities and cramped seating, the future of Fenway has been questioned for years. Like the struggle that raged over the fate of Detroit's Tiger Stadium, Red Sox owners and fans have argued over whether to renovate Fenway Park or vacate it. In the late 1990s, Red Sox officials went so far as to release plans for a new multimillion-dollar park that would be an exact replica of Fenway Park, with all the modern amenities added. Fortunately for all concerned, that went nowhere.

In 2002, Fenway was given new life when the Red Sox were sold to an ownership group sensitive to the park's historic stature. New team owner John Henry has said that Fenway's fate is up in the air, but that his first choice is a "major renovation." Given that Fenway is the most consistently sold-out park in the majors, this seems like a good balance between conserving a historic ballpark, accommodating a modern, expanding fan base.

OPPOSITE: *One of the smallest parks in the major leagues, Boston's beloved Fenway never has a problem with empty seats.* **BELOW:** *Towering 37 feet (11.3m) high, Fenway Park's Green Monster has been taunting hitters for more than fifty years. To the left of the scoreboard is the only in-play ladder in the major leagues.*

BUILD THE HOUSE THAT MERCY NEEDS... SUPPORT BROOKLYN RED CROSS BUILDING FUND

THE CLASSIC ERA, 1900–1960

Ebbets Field
Brooklyn (1913–57)

Built on the site of a garbage yard known as Pigtown, Ebbets Field turned a dump into a palace of baseball, and after its demise, into an urban legend. "Of all the ballparks that no longer exist," wrote Lawrence Ritter in his classic book *Lost Ballparks*, "none have been romanticized more than Ebbets Field."

The lost Mecca of ballparks, Ebbets Field had physical characteristics so recognizable that they've become stereotypes. The small dimensions of Ebbets Field enabled fans to be so close to the game they were, in the words of announcer Red Barber, "practically an infielder." The park's home run fences were peppered with advertisements, including clothier Abe Stark's legendary billboard that read, "Hit sign, win suit." And if you're looking for the inspiration for the brick facades of San Francisco's Pacific Bell Park or Baltimore's Camden Yards, look no further than Ebbets Field, whose magnificent brick entrance tempted the faithful into an Italian marble rotunda. The floor tiles represented the stitches on a baseball, and from the 27-foot (8m) ceiling hung a chandelier with twelve baseball-bat arms, each holding baseball-shaped globes.

Longing to move out of Washington Park, a cramped firetrap that the Dodgers called home, owner Charles Ebbet built the new jewel in 1913. Ebbet believed the baseball fan should be "taken care of" and sunk $750,000, an obscene amount of money for the day, into his new edifice. But before it was done, Ebbet had to sell half his interest in the team to pay for it.

The original park consisted of double-decked grandstands extending 30 feet (9m) past the infield, and holding

LEFT: *Duke Snider belts one over the Ebbets Field scoreboard during the first game of the 1952 World Series.*

BELOW: *A Dodger yearbook from 1954, depicting the team's dream of a new stadium. Three years later they got their wish with a move to Los Angeles.*

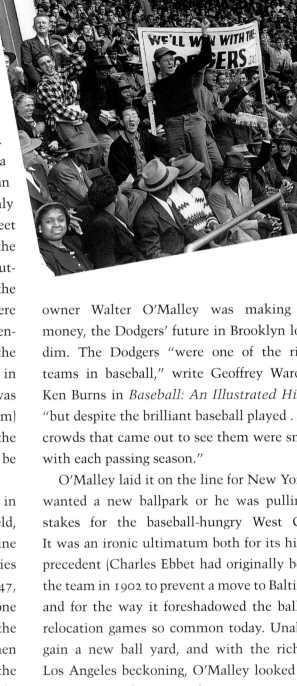

BELOW: *Dodger Duke Snider lunges for a ball against the fence at Ebbets Field in 1954.* **RIGHT:** *The Brooklyn faithful cheer for their beloved "Bums."*

OPPOSITE: *Future Hall of Famer Jackie Robinson walks home from Ebbets Field on April 16, 1947, just one day after he broke the color barrier.*

just 25,000 people. After the the 1931 season the grandstands were expanded to increase capacity to 32,000. The right-field wall and scoreboard was said to have more than 289 different angles, and playing the outfield at Ebbets was reputed to be so tricky that tips were passed on through generations of Dodger fielders.

Ebbets Field was initially a pitcher's park. Upon completion in 1913, center field was a distant 450 feet (137m), and ballooned to an unachievable 466 feet (142m) in 1930. The only manageable fence was right field, at 301 feet (92m). Gradually over the years, though, as more out-field seating was added, the home run distances were reduced to mortal dimen-sions, and by the 1940s the center field had come in 50 feet (15m). Right field was topped by a 38-foot (11.5m) fence, and balls hitting the fence were considered to be in play.

The Dodgers prospered in their years at Ebbets Field, winning the pennant nine times and the World Series once. But on April 15, 1947, Ebbets Field gave fans one of the greatest thrills in the history of the game, when Jackie Robinson took the field for the Dodgers, break-ing the game's infamous color barrier, and marking the beginning of the end of baseball's deepest travesty.

Brooklynites loved their ballpark and their team, whom they affectionately called "Dem Bums." But in the end, even though Dodger

owner Walter O'Malley was making good money, the Dodgers' future in Brooklyn looked dim. The Dodgers "were one of the richest teams in baseball," write Geoffrey Ward and Ken Burns in *Baseball: An Illustrated History*, "but despite the brilliant baseball played . . . the crowds that came out to see them were smaller with each passing season."

O'Malley laid it on the line for New York: he wanted a new ballpark or he was pulling up stakes for the baseball-hungry West Coast. It was an ironic ultimatum both for its historic precedent (Charles Ebbet had originally bought the team in 1902 to prevent a move to Baltimore) and for the way it foreshadowed the ballpark-relocation games so common today. Unable to gain a new ball yard, and with the riches of Los Angeles beckoning, O'Malley looked to go west. In 1957 the National League owners voted to allow him to do just that.

The Dodgers played their last game at Ebbets Field on September 24, 1957, and only 6,702 people bothered to show up. A few years later, on February 23, 1960, Lucy Monroe sang the national anthem at Ebbets Field, just as she had many times before. Moments later, a two-ton wrecking ball brought down Ebbets Field and broke the heart of Brooklyn.

ABOVE: *Even without a recent World Series, there's plenty of baseball history on Chicago's north side: Sammy Sosa slams his sixty-second home run of the year at Wrigley Field on September 13, 1998.*

Wrigley Field
Chicago (opened 1914)

To most baseball fans, ballparks begin and end with Wrigley Field. From its ivy-covered walls to its timeless manually operated scoreboard, Wrigley Field is the standard against which today's new "retro" ballparks are judged. The home of the Chicago Cubs is the second oldest ballpark in the majors, preceded only by Boston's Fenway Park (built in 1912).

Wrigley was built in 1914 by restaurant magnate Charlie Weeghman, who housed his Federal League Chicago Whales there until the upstart league went belly-up in 1915. Weeghman put together an investor group, bought the Chicago Cubs from the Taft family of Cincinnati, and moved the team to his two-year-old ballpark on the corner of Clark and Addison on Chicago's north side. The Cubs played their first game at the park in April 1916.

Weeghman Park, as Wrigley was then known, was a modest little park, holding only 14,000 and costing a mere $250,000 to build. By 1920 chewing-gum king William Wrigley, Jr., had bought out Weeghman and changed the name to Cubs Park, and in 1926 to Wrigley Field. That same year the grandstands were doubled and the capacity blossomed to more than 38,000.

In 1937 the outfield grandstands were erected and a new, bright-green scoreboard went up, ordered by Bill Veeck, who would later invent the exploding scoreboard across town at Comiskey Park. Operated by a team of ladder-climbing number-posters, this new technical marvel featured in-progress scores and pitcher's numbers. The numbers indicating batter, ball, strike, and out, along with "H" and "E" to signify hit and miss, were shaped like eyes. A mechanical clock was added to the top of the scoreboard in 1941. Traditional yet imposing, the 25- by 75-foot (7.6x23m) Wrigley Field scoreboard is considered the standard by which all other scoreboards are judged. It has passed the test of time, and lumber. To this day, no batter has hit

it, although Roberto Clemente and Bill Nicholson have come close.

Outfield bleachers were added in 1937 and Veeck, inspired by the ivy walls he had seen at a stadium in Indianapolis, ordered trees and plants in center field. In all, 350 Japanese bittersweet plants and 200 Boston ivy plants were planted, as well as 8 Chinese elm trees in pots on the bleacher steps. But the fierce Lake Michigan wind soon made twigs of the trees, and the bittersweet plants bit the dust as well. The ivy survived, however, and continues to cover the outfield walls to this day. In fact, the house rules at Wrigley Field even provide for the ivy, as any ball that gets stuck in the vines is a ground-rule double.

Wrigley is a field of firsts. In 1941 the Cubs became the first major league team to serenade their fans with organ music. Wrigley was the first park where fans could keep balls hit for home runs, but it is also where fans started throwing back opponent's home run balls. And when fans complained of vendors blocking their view, Wrigley was the first park to construct permanent concession stands.

This Chicago landmark has seen its share of historic events, but none more so than Babe Ruth's historic "called shot" in the 1932 World Series. Although it has long been debated whether Ruth actually telegraphed his dinger, there's no doubt that Ruth gave a gesture to center field right before slamming one out. Intentional or not, journalists had a field day, one saying Ruth "pointed to the spot where he expected to send his rapier home." Many years later, even Ruth himself questioned whether he actually called the shot, but the resulting homer is one of the many historic legacies of Wrigley Field.

Wrigley Field has changed delightfully little since its early days. In fact, Wrigley was the last ballpark in the majors to install lights—it was day games only until 1988, when Major League Baseball threatened to make the Cubs play post-

WRIGLEY FIELD
1947
NATIONAL LEAGUE STARS
AMERICAN LEAGUE STARS
ALBERT B. CHANDLER
Commissioner of Baseball
Lower Grand Stand $3.00
Est. Price 2.50 — Fed. Tax .50
Right reserved to refund price and revoke
license granted
by this ticket.

PLAYED FOR THE BENEFIT OF
MAJOR LEAGUE BASEBALL
PLAYERS' PENSION FUND

UNDER THE AUSPICES OF
THE SIXTEEN MAJOR LEAGUE
BASEBALL CLUBS
Chicago National League Ball Club

DID NOT DELIVER THIS STUB
FROM MAIN CHECK

WRIGLEY FIELD
1947
NATIONAL LEAGUE STARS
AMERICAN LEAGUE STARS
RAIN CHECK
LOWER
GRAND STAND $3.00
Est. Price 2.50 Fed. Tax .50

RETAIN THIS CHECK
NOT GOOD IF DETACHED

TORCO

season ball in St. Louis unless lights were installed. But even that bit of modernization has done little to diminish the charm of Wrigley.

Chicago ferociously loves the Cubs and their crown jewel of a ballpark. On any game day the city streets surrounding the park can look more like Mardi Gras than Chicago's north side. Maybe it's just blind optimism, since the Cubs have never won a World Series in Wrigley (their last was 1908, six years before Wrigley was built). As longtime fan and Chicago native Doug McConnell tells it, "Walk onto Addison Street after a Friday-night Cub victory, with mobs of people and bands playing in the street, and you'd think they'd won the World Series!"

TOP: *Ticket to the 1947 All-Star game held at Wrigley Field.*
CENTER: *Wrigley's trademark ivy-covered outfield walls are among the park's most distinctive characteristics.* **BOTTOM:** *Wrigley Field remains very much the same as it was when it opened in 1914, to the delight of baseball fans of all stripes.*
NEXT PAGE: *Chicago's Wrigley Field packed with fans in 2001, the year Sammy Sosa slugged sixty-four homers for the Cubs.*

Yankee Stadium

New York (opened 1923)

Some ballparks are beautiful buildings, architectural monuments whose palatial surroundings inspire and awe. Other ballparks stand out for the historic games and fantastic athletes they have showcased. For the combination of heavenly events and hallowed halls, no other ball yard holds a candle to Yankee Stadium. Peering onto the field from the grandstand gives one an overwhelming feeling, an immense appreciation of both the stadium itself and the players it has seen.

The Yankee dynasty at East 161st Street and River Avenue in the Bronx actually started before a single shovel of dirt was turned over. In fact, the origins of pinstripe domination date back to 1919, when the Yankees acquired Babe Ruth from the Red Sox. At that time the Yankees shared the Polo Grounds with the Giants, an arrangement in effect since 1913. But with the slugging Ruth in tow, the Yankees were not only starting to dominate the standings, they were pulling in the crowds as well. The Polo Grounds' slugger-friendly home run fences left home run territory wide open, and Ruth's frequent homers were soon stealing the show in New York.

And so out Ruth went, along with the rest of the team, with an eviction notice served by the Giants in 1921 (the Yanks vacated after the 1922 season). So intense was their rivalry that Giants owners were willing to do just about anything in their quest for victory, even trying to force the Yankees out of business. "If we kick them out they won't be able to find another location on Manhattan Island," the Giants' John McGraw said at the time. "The fans will forget about them and they will be through."

But banishment to the Bronx, on the other side of the Harlem River, was far from a fatal blow for the Yankees, who finished their massive new ballpark in time for the 1923 season. To the contrary, it gave them an edifice in proportion to their growing legacy. The first ballpark to be called a "stadium," Yankee Stadium

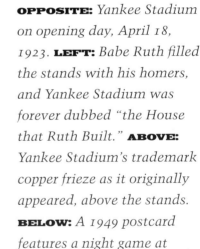

OPPOSITE: *Yankee Stadium on opening day, April 18, 1923.* **LEFT:** *Babe Ruth filled the stands with his homers, and Yankee Stadium was forever dubbed "the House that Ruth Built."* **ABOVE:** *Yankee Stadium's trademark copper frieze as it originally appeared, above the stands.* **BELOW:** *A 1949 postcard features a night game at Yankee Stadium.*

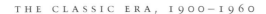

ABOVE: *Program from the 1941 World Series.* BELOW: *All of Yankee Stadium pays tribute to Babe Ruth during a ceremony to retire his uniform number in June 1948. This was to be the last time the Babe would wear Yankee pinstripes, as he passed away two months later.*

was a triple-deck marvel that held 58,000 fans. The top deck was adorned with a distinctive copper frieze, which became an icon of Yankee Stadium.

From day one, Yankee Stadium was an enormous success. Opening day on April 18, 1923, saw John Philip Sousa lead a military band, and Babe Ruth hit the first home run. An *Evening Telegram* writer was so convinced of Ruth's history-making potential in his new home, he dubbed the stadium "the House that Ruth Built" and the name stuck.

Like most ballparks of its era, the original Yankee Stadium had outfield dimensions that were massive, and sometimes bizarre. Left-center field was 500 feet (152m) from home plate and deemed "Death Valley" by those unfortunate hitters trying to slug into it. In 1923 the right-field foul line and bleachers met at such an acute angle it was dubbed the "Blood Angle" for the pain right fielders experienced trying to track down a ball hit there. In case that wasn't tricky enough for batters, center field featured a flag pole in fair territory.

In 1932 a stone monument to the great Yankee manager Miller Huggins was erected in center field, followed by monuments to Lou Gehrig in 1941 and Babe Ruth in 1949. Located in fair territory, these monuments complicated plays, and sometimes even made frustrated managers evoke Yankee ghosts. Yankee manager Casey Stengel once watched with frustration as his center fielder lost a ball among the monuments, and yelled, "Ruth, Gehrig, Huggins, someone throw that darned ball in here *now!*"

The next decades saw many minor alterations to Yankee Stadium, and many more monumental baseball moments. During the 1920s and 1930s, second and third decks were added in the outfield, and wooden bleachers were replaced with concrete. As a result, center field was pulled in over 30 feet (9m) in 1937, and addi-

tional scoreboards appeared in the '40s.

While the park evolved, the games it witnessed made history. Yankee Stadium saw a home run record set by Babe Ruth in 1927, and again by Roger Maris in 1961. Don Larsen pitched a perfect World Series game there in 1956, and Yankee Stadium saw the farewell of a succession of great champions, including Ruth, Lou Gehrig, Joe DiMaggio, and Mickey Mantle.

By the 1970s time had caught up with the old ballpark, and Yankee owners contemplated becoming the New Jersey Yankees. So, while the Yankees took up residence in Shea Stadium, the ballpark underwent a major renovation in 1974 and 1975. The monuments were moved behind left-center field, and gone was the charming practice of allowing fans to exit the stadium through center field. The distinctive copper frieze that had lined the stadium was moved to a portion of center field. Armed with a new stadium, the Yankees ended the 1970s on a tear, with a dominating team that included Reggie "Mr. October" Jackson, who hit three home runs on three pitches during the 1977 World Series.

The last decade of the twentieth century saw some grumblings about Yankee Stadium from owner George Steinbrenner. There was even a plan floated for a new park in Manhattan. But with the economic downturn of the new millennium and the September 11 terrorist attacks, New York found itself with more pressing financial needs, so this venerable landmark of New York history will stand as it is for now.

Not that you'll hear any fans complaining. Yankee Stadium pulled in the highest average attendance of all major league parks in 2003, attracting over 42,000 fans per game. Not many parks, old or new, can boast that kind of fan appreciation. Of course, with a team that won twenty-six World Series championships in the twentieth century, what's not to appreciate? In an era of newer and better ballparks, it looks like there will be no nails pulled from "The House That Ruth Built."

ABOVE: *Yankee Stadium after the renovation of 1974–75. Notice the copper frieze was moved to the outfield.*

LEFT: *The retired numbers of Yankee greats line the walls of Yankee Stadium's Memorial Park.*

CHAPTER 2

The Modern Era, 1960–1990

By 1960 many of America's major league ballparks were considerably out of step with the times. Unfortunately, the predictable rhythm of organ music on a sunny afternoon in a small urban park was simply not meeting the modern needs of postwar society. Newly affluent mobile families looked to pack the kids into their cars and head to the ballgame. This meant two things: more seats and more parking, which dictated larger parks located outside congested city centers. It also meant that games were played at night, something for which many classic ballparks were not prepared. Profit-hungry owners looked to appease the masses, forgoing tradition in the interest of progress. By the time the Dodgers

OPPOSITE: *Toronto's ultramodern SkyDome, standing in the shadows of the massive CN Tower.*

ABOVE: *Pro Player Stadium in Miami, home of the Florida Marlins.* **OPPOSITE:** *It's not just for baseball any more: the all-weather Toronto SkyDome is billed as "The World's Greatest Entertainment Centre."*

and the Giants headed west in search of new stadiums, the pattern was clear: baseball was changing forever.

The modern era saw the lowly baseball park morph into a modern giant (many would say nightmare). Capacities often boomed up to 60,000—too great a number to enable anyone to appreciate the nuances of the game. Architectural character took a back seat to perceived functionality, as the new ballpark became a strictly utilitarian object. Gone were the cherished brick facades of the urban jewels. Towering ovals of concrete now dominated baseball's landscape. Artificial turf, first used as a Band-Aid solution when the Astrodome's roof kept out the sun and killed the natural grass, became both a groundskeeping practicality and a slap in the face of tradition.

As for permanence, the numbers speak for themselves. From 1960 to 1990, eighteen new major league ballparks went up in America,

starting with Candlestick Park in 1960. By the end of the century, almost 30 percent of these yards were replaced. And of the remaining parks, only a few, such as Dodger Stadium, look as though they might withstand the test of time.

It would be too easy to look back at the ballparks of the 1960s and 1970s and dismiss them as poorly planned mistakes, although many of them were. More significantly, the era was an incredible learning period for today's ballpark architect. As the old cliché goes, you don't know what you've got until it's gone. The modern era saw the death of Ebbets Field and the Polo Grounds, both urban legends. But it also saw the demise of such lesser-known gems as Forbes Field in Pittsburgh and Crosley Field in Cincinnati, both replaced by larger-than-life stadiums. These parks can never be brought back, and we can only hope that when new sandlots go up in the future, there will be a liberal application of lessons learned.

Candlestick Park
San Francisco (1960–99)

Candlestick Park is universally identified by one singular, defining characteristic. No, it's not Willie Mays's 3,000th hit, which he got at Candlestick on July 18, 1971, nor the back-to-back no-hitters thrown by the Giants' Gaylord Perry and the Cardinals' Ray Washburn on September 17 and 18, 1968. It isn't even the massive earthquake that shook the 62,000 fans who were watching the Giants play their Bay Area neighbors, the Oakland A's, in the World Series on October 17, 1989. More than anything else, Candlestick will always be remembered for one thing: atrocious weather.

Located in one of the coldest, foggiest parts of San Francisco, Candlestick became legendary for the ferocious winds that swirl around this concrete park, causing dust storms in the infield, turning home runs into pop flies, and making peanut wrappers hover in midair. One of the more enduring legends of Candlestick has Giants pitcher Stu Miller being blown off the mound during the 1961 All-Star game. (Miller later denied being tossed, saying the wind "just threw me off a little.") Dubbed "Candle-fridge" by some locals, night games are so cold that fans surviving extra-inning night games have been awarded a special "Croix de Candlestick" pin.

As a part of baseball's California gold rush of the 1950s, New York Giants owner Horace Stoneham decided to move his Giants to San Francisco after the city agreed to build him a 40,000–seat stadium with 12,000 parking spots. A plot of land on the outskirts of the city, called Candlestick Point for the jagged rocks and trees that covered it, was deemed appropriate after a splendid midmorning tour of the site by Stoneham and the mayor of San Francisco. Of course, the notorious Candlestick wind never cropped up till afternoon, so the supposedly placid site was chosen.

Almost immediately the problems began. Architect John Bolles was chosen, even though he had never designed a ballpark. The original plans called for heating pipes to run under half of the seats, but when the builders installed them five inches (12.7cm) into the concrete rather than one inch (2.54cm), the system became useless. (In 1962, maverick San Francisco lawyer Melvin Belli sued the city for the cost of his season tickets, claiming he had paid for seats that were supposed to be toasty warm, and won.)

But even grand jury investigations into the project didn't stop Candlestick from rising, and on April 12, 1960, the park opened. Foreshadowing a brand of foot-in-mouth tactics that would later bring his term to a premature end, President Richard Nixon dedicated Candlestick, calling it "one of the most beautiful ballparks of all time."

Originally a concrete horseshoe, Candlestick suffered badly from the winds, which not only froze the faithful in the stands but hampered play on the field. It has been said that if Willie Mays (who hit 660 career homers) hadn't spent so many seasons at Candlestick, he and not Hank Aaron might be the all-time home run king.

With the new San Francisco 49ers looking to share the yard, the stadium was enclosed into a concrete oval in 1971. But the new design only served to create a wind tunnel in the stadium, and a massive challenge in fielding the ball. After trying to catch pop flies at Candlestick, Dodger shortstop Dave Anderson said, "You look like one of those guys in the circus balancing poles." The new design also increased the seating capacity to an astonishing 62,000, with upper-level seating seemingly miles from home plate. Artificial turf was installed the same year, and most of the resemblance to a traditional ballpark had vanished.

One of the best Candlestick horror stories comes from player-turned-manager Phil Garner: "I remember one day when I was playing third base for the Pirates and I called for a pop fly between the bag and the mound," Garner told the *Milwaukee Journal Sentinel* in 1999. "I'm coming in toward the mound to catch the ball and Willie Stargell ends up catching it in foul territory on the other side of first base!"

THE MODERN ERA, 1960–1990

Candlestick saw few improvements over the years, the most noticeable being the reintroduction of a natural grass field in 1979. All the while, a succession of Giants owners struggled over what to do with their dismay on the bay. Numerous public referendums were put before San Francisco voters, who consistently voted down the use of public money in the construction of a new Giants ballpark. But in March 1996, San Francisco finally gave its approval for the construction of a new Giants ballpark, one that would be built without the use of public money for construction. With this vote, the Giants ushered in a new economic era for ballparks, one in which the people who come to the game—and not the general public—foot the bill.

San Francisco's new confines, SBC Park, opened in spring 2000 as the first privately funded ballpark built for Major League Baseball since Dodger Stadium first swung upen its gates in 1962. In the meantime, Candlestick endures, filling the need for which it's probaby best suited: as a home for football.

OPPOSITE: *Candlestick Park, which the Giants abandoned in 2000, was universally hated for its cavernous interior and atrocious weather.*

ABOVE: *Confusion reigns at Candlestick Park after an earthquake on October 17, 1989. Although game three of the World Series was cancelled, the massive concrete ballpark withstood the quake, and the series resumed nine days later.*

Dodger Stadium
Los Angeles (opened 1962)

Popping up at the advent of the modern ballpark era, Dodger stadium is a true anomaly. In an era when large, impersonal stadiums ruled, and when sharing a stadium with football was a universal truth, Dodger Stadium emerged as one of the most perfect baseball environments ever constructed. More surprising, it continues to shine even today, since very little has changed with this pristine masterpiece in the past three and a half decades.

Rewind to 1957. The Dodgers have just announced their heartbreaking departure from Brooklyn and are perusing Los Angeles in search of a location for their new ballpark. After a helicopter ride over the city, Dodger owner Walter O'Malley fancied a 315–acre (126ha) area called Chavez Ravine, conveniently located between Pasadena and downtown Los Angeles. Close to freeways and with enough room for acres of parking, Chavez Ravine was perfect for O'Malley's modern ballpark.

Even though the land had been previously earmarked for public use, trouble started almost immediately as residents of the area called foul and refused to move. Things got ugly as squatters dug in their heels. By the spring of 1959 the

BELOW: *Dodger Ron Cey battles the Yankees in the 1978 World Series at Dodger Stadium.* OPPOSITE: *In the age of ugly suburban ballparks, pristine Dodger Stadium somehow got it right.*

sheriff came in to forcibly evict stubborn residents, who had set up a tent city. But in the end O'Malley was able to buy out most of the last remaining holdouts in Chavez Ravine to make room for his new ballpark. Later that year the site was cleared, and construction started on what would be the first privately financed ballpark since Yankee Stadium went up in 1923.

Dodger Stadium debuted on April 10, 1962, and the bar for ballpark excellence was raised considerably. With parking for 16,000 automobiles spread out on twenty-one terraced lots, Dodger Stadium was seen as a modern marvel. The new park boasted more than 3,400 trees among its 300 acres (120ha) of landscaping, with breathtaking views of the San Gabriel Mountains and the emerging downtown skyline. A far cry from the gritty urban scenes of East Coast ballparks, Dodger Stadium boldly flaunted a new brand of California baseball. To this day Dodger Stadium is meticulously manicured, and is still one of the most pristine ballparks in the major leagues.

Immaculate Dodger Stadium in Los Angeles, where the outfield ads are one of the few changes this ballpark has seen over the years.

Inside, one cannot imagine a better setting for baseball. Although it holds 56,000 fans, Dodger Stadium is deceptively intimate, with perfect sight lines and logical proportions. Every inch is designed with the fan in mind, right down to the open concourse, where fans can watch the game while waiting in line for food. Even the stadium's symmetrical dimensions, while not "retro" in feel, give the park a sense of order that seems surprisingly appropriate.

From the beginning Dodger Stadium brought success to the box office, and to the field. Since moving into their new palace, the Dodgers have hosted eight World Series and won four, beginning with a 1963 victory just one year after the yard opened. And in the attendance department, the Dodgers are consistently at the top of the standings. In 1978 Dodger Stadium was the first ballpark to host more than three million fans in a season, and has done so twelve times since.

Not a group to mess with perfection, the Dodger organization has made few changes to the stadium since its construction. The original

plans for the park called for a huge fountain in center field, and the structure was designed so that the upper decks could wrap around into the familiar "doughnut" shape, bringing the capacity to a staggering 85,000 seats. But in the end, the Dodger organizational culture prevailed, and like most other aspects of the team up to 1998, the stadium wasn't touched. Kudos to the Dodgers: Dodger Stadium is the only pre-1990 ballpark that has never changed its capacity.

Many exciting things have happened at Dodger Stadium over the years, but change was rarely one of them. In the last four decades of the twentieth century, the Dodger organization and their untarnished park became famous for perennial stability and success. It is ironic that the O'Malley family, the owners who were despised for taking the Dodgers out of Brooklyn, created a franchise in Los Angeles that became the standard-bearer for baseball tradition.

In 1998, the O'Malley family shocked the base-ball world by selling the Los Angeles Dodgers to Rupert Murdoch's Fox Group, ending the era of family ownership in baseball. Although few changes had been made to Dodger Stadium throughout the years, the 1999 off-season brought more luxury suites and expanded dugout boxes, all as part of an effort to bring in more revenue. Concerned fans feared that this was the beginning of the end for the Dodger Stadium they knew and loved. But in 2003, the Dodgers' ownership changed again, and Dodger Stadium still stands. With a park this perfect, who would dare do more than tinker? In the ever-changing world of the baseball business, anything is possible, but one thing remains certain: little can change the overall appeal of Dodger Stadium, which is as timeless as the game itself.

The Houston Astrodome, whose light-blocking dome led to the creation of Astroturf.

Astrodome
Houston (1965–99)

With a fully enclosed dome measuring eighteen stories high, an artificial playing surface, and central air-conditioning pumping out 2.5 million cubic feet of air per minute, the Astrodome personified the era of big, multipurpose stadiums. While the rest of the baseball world also envisioned ballparks that were "multipurpose," it took the Texans to outdo everybody. Love it or hate it, there's no denying that the Astrodome was the most ostentatious flip ever to baseball tradition.

Astro owner Judge Roy Hofheinz (previously Lyndon Johnson's campaign manager) had been bitten by the geodesic dome bug of the '60s while trying to build a domed shopping mall. But after his Houston Colt .45s were awarded a National League expansion franchise, Hofheinz set his sites on the most outlandish park in the majors. By the time he was finished, the Astrodome included padded seats, futuristic "Sky Boxes," and an exploding scoreboard.

Hofheinz called his concrete marvel the "Eighth Wonder of the World" but after the first exhibition game, with the Yankees in April 1965, players were more likely to exclaim, "I wonder where the ball is!" It turned out that the translucent cream-colored panels of the dome were great for letting light into the stadium, but murder when it came to seeing fly balls. The Astro owner had a big problem on his hands, and went to great lengths to solve it. "When outfielders insisted they couldn't see the ball and several players called the conditions dangerous, Hofheinz handed out orange sunglasses," wrote author Michael Gershman in *Diamonds: The Evolution of the Ballparks*. "In self-defense, the outfielders began wearing batting helmets during games. The Astros tried ten dozen balls dyed several colors—yellow, orange, red and cerise—to no avail."

The ultimate solution solved one problem, caused another, and changed the course of ballparks for thirty years. To alleviate the glare, the roof panels were painted. But the lack of natural light made the grass die, so they tried painting the grass green. You can guess how that turned out. Finally, the Monsanto company was commissioned to come up with an artificial surface, and Astroturf was born. Controversial from the beginning, artificial turf would soon become common among new ballparks. And while owners loved the economics of the reduced groundskeeping, the new plastic grass had few advocates among baseball players. "If horses won't eat it," infielder Dick Allen once said, "I won't play on it."

For the next thirty-five years, no event was too big for the Astrodome. Evel Knievel used it to perform a world-record motorcycle jump, Billie Jean King beat Bobby Riggs there, and Elvis Presley performed his final concert at the Astrodome. But eventually time caught up to the Astros' fancy home. Even after a $60 million expansion in 1989, the star-studded dome lost its glitter, and Astro owner Drayton McLane, Jr., threatened to take his team to Virginia unless he got a new park. As a result, 1999 was the final season for baseball in the Astrodome, which was to be replaced by Minute Maid Park, a spanking new stadium with a retractable roof. As reporter John Williams noted in the *Houston Chronicle*, "Goodbye, dome sweet dome; hello poptop."

ABOVE: *No sun and artificial turf: the Astrodome shocked the baseball world when it opened in 1965.*

PAGES 70–71: *When it opened, the Astrodome was billed as "The Eighth Wonder of the World."*

The "Concrete Doughnuts"

The infamous troika of "concrete doughnuts." **BELOW:** *Busch Stadium, St. Louis, Missouri.* **OPPOSITE TOP:** *Three Rivers Stadium in Pittsburgh, Pennsylvania.* **OPPOSITE BOTTOM:** *Veterans Stadium, Philadelphia, Pennsylvania.*

Through the 1960s and 1970s many of the charming old parks of the early century were being traded in for "multipurpose" concrete stadiums, most of which lacked the distinguishing architectural characteristics so common in earlier parks. But starting in the late '60s a new crop of ballparks sprang up that were so similar in design, it was difficult to tell them apart. In a five-year period from 1966 to 1971, cookie-cutter parks popped up in Atlanta, St. Louis, Pittsburgh, Cincinnati, and Philadelphia, all virtually identical. "I stand at the plate," Pirates third baseman Richie Hebner once said of these clones, "and I honestly don't know whether I'm in Pittsburgh, Cincinnati, St. Louis, or Philly. They all look alike."

Dubbed by some as being the dark age of ballparks, the late '60s yielded a crop of stadiums that were a direct affront to baseball's sensibilities. These new parks were a slap in the face of tradition, evidenced by the fact that all of them sported artificial turf when they opened. It's unclear what is more startling about these ball yards: the fact that they are so strikingly similar, or the fact that such heinous mistakes could be so blithely duplicated.

Nicknamed the "concrete doughnuts," these multilevel, oval-shaped stadiums were considered the future of baseball. Of course, no one could have predicted that there would be such backlash against these monstrosities that every one would be vacated in a scant three decades.

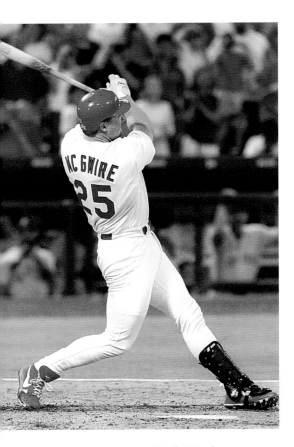

ABOVE: *With Mark McGwire breaking records in St. Louis, Cardinal fans pile into Busch Stadium.*

BELOW: *A postcard depicting Sportsman's Park, home of the St. Louis Cardinals from 1920 to 1966.*

Busch Stadium
St. Louis (opened 1966)

Busch Stadium holds the distinction of being the one concrete doughnut that was given a chance. Despite the stadium's large capacity and bland architecture, St. Louis remained satisfied with its concrete oval far longer than other doughnut cities. The Cardinals did a good job of putting fans in the seats with a number of well-timed improvements to the park. But more than these improvements, the historic events unfolding on the field extended the life of Busch Stadium far longer than anyone could have imagined.

A little history: Sportsman's Park housed the St. Louis Cardinals from 1920 to 1966, and before that, the St. Louis Browns from 1902 until their departure to Baltimore in 1953. By the late 1960s, Sportsman's Park was showing its age, and St. Louis started to plan for a new ballpark as part of a downtown rejuvenation project. On May 8, 1966, the Cardinals played their last game at Sportsman's Park—renamed Busch Stadium in 1953 after the beer dynasty that bought the team—and immediately afterward a helicopter transported home plate to the Cardinals new home, also called Busch Stadium. The Cardinals inaugurated their new ballpark with a twelve-inning win over the Atlanta Braves on May 12, 1966.

Busch Stadium sits within spitting distance of the famous St. Louis arch, and features an arch design of its own along its roofline. A triple-decked concrete marvel, Busch Stadium ushered in a new era of monolith stadiums that were quickly copied, with three nearly identical structures built soon afterward around the country.

Like other parks of the era, Busch Stadium rushed to install artificial turf. But in a unique move, the base paths were left dirt, giving the park a more traditional feel. (Candlestick Park was the only other stadium to mix traditional dirt base paths with artificial turf, in 1971.) That didn't last long, however, and by 1977 the dirt "patches" at each base and the pitcher's mound were all that remained.

Unlike many of the other cookie-cutter parks, Busch Stadium saw a series of improvements over the years. When the St. Louis Cardinals football team, which shared the stadium, split for Phoenix in the late '80s, Busch Stadium got some much needed baseball-only renovations. In 1987 every seat was replaced, and the sound and video systems got a big upgrade in 1993. By 1996, Busch Stadium, in a retro upgrade, nixed the wall-to-wall AstroTurf carpeting and went back to a natural playing surface. Adding to that old-time flavor, a hand-operated scoreboard was installed in 1997.

That same year, the Cardinals acquired a stocky first baseman with red hair and a reputation for landing on the disabled list. It was soon obvious, however, that Mark McGwire was more than a slugger with Popeye forearms—he was the future of Cardinals baseball. In 1998, the faithful swarmed through the gates of Busch Stadium to watch McGwire make a run at the single-season home run record, and tear it to shreds. By now, everyone knows that McGwire would go on to knock out seventy homers in 1998, breaking Roger Maris' 1961 record of sixty-one homers. McGwire also shattered the National Leage record for most home runs at home (thirty-eight), breaking Ted Kluszewski's 1954 record of thirty-four. Despite what amounts to a park fans should hate, Busch Stadium has done remarkably

well. St. Louis fans, famous for their sports fanaticism, flocked to their concrete-oval yard. As late as 2001, Busch Stadium pulled in more than three million fans, and even in the economically depressed year of 2003, the old park brought in over 35,000 fans per game.

Even with all the effort it's taken to keep Busch Stadium above water, it looks like it's going to go under. In spring 2003, the Cardinals announced plans for a new $650 million "baseball village," one of the largest development projects in St. Louis history. And while you can't blame St. Louis fans for wanting to send their old concrete stadium to the wrecking ball, you've got to admit it'll go down swinging.

The St. Louis skyline and the famous arch peer down over Busch Stadium.

Cinergy Field (formerly Riverfront Stadium)

Cincinnati (opened 1970)

For almost six decades Cincinnati's venerable Crosley Field was the home for the city's Reds. But in the early '60s the old stadium began to show its age in more ways than one. Of course, there were the usual complaints of outdated facilities and small capacity (Crosley held just 29,488 fans). But two important developments spelled the death of Cincinnati's old ballpark.

First was the westward tide that was sweeping baseball teams to the coast. The Dodgers and the Giants were caught up and headed west, and other West Coast cites went fishing for prospects.

In the early '60s the city of San Diego lobbied hard for the Reds, offering to build a state-of-the-art ballpark. Having witnessed the demoralization that occurred in New York when two of their three teams left town, Cincinnati was hell-bent not to lose the Reds.

But the death blow to Crosley was professional football, which was growing by leaps and bounds in the '60s. Cincinnati was awarded a professional football franchise in 1966. With that announcement, the city became the next victim of the regrettable trend of multipurpose stadiums, and a new stadium was planned on the Ohio River.

On June 24, 1970, the Reds beat the Giants 5–4 in their last game at Crosley Field, and less

RIGHT: *Crosley Field, home of the Cincinnati Reds from 1912 to 1970, featured an incline in the outfield, making a fielder's dash to the wall an uphill trek.* **BELOW:** *Palace of The Fans in 1905, the second of five Cincinnati major league parks.*

than a week later they landed in their spanking-new concrete doughnut. Although it uses the old home plate from Crosley Field, little else of Riverfront Stadium bears much resemblance to traditional ballparks.

Triple-decked all around, Riverfront saw many regrettable firsts. Taking artificial turf to the extreme, Riverfront was the first stadium to carpet the base paths, leaving dirt patches only at the bases, the pitcher's mound, and home plate. Riverfront Stadium also saw the first World Series on artificial turf when the Reds hosted the 1970 fall classic against Baltimore.

The Reds saw many great baseball moments in their concrete tub on the river, including the heyday of the "Big Red Machine" in the '70s. But with the stratospheric baseball salaries of the '80s and '90s, economic realities took a toll at the ticket booth. By 2002, Cincinnati's alba-

tross was drawing only a little more than 23,000 fans per game at Riverfront (by this time renamed Cinergy Field after a corporate name sell-off). While the boys from Cincinnati visited the World Series four times in the '70s, they only appeared once from 1980 to 2000.

To no one's surprise, the team spent the last years of the twentieth century pushing for a new ballpark. In 2001, a large section of the outfield was removed from Cinergy Field to make room for the construction of Great American Ball Park. After spending its last couple of years torn open with its successor waiting just beyond its home run fences, Cinergy Field was imploded on December 29, 2002. Great American Ball Park opened in 2003, and although budget constraints have kept this new park from being the gem that other new parks are, it's leagues above the cavernous Riverfront Stadium.

ABOVE: *A commemorative belt buckle from Cincinnati's first ballpark, later renamed Crosley Field.* **BELOW:** *An archetypal modern-era stadium, Cincinatti's Cinergy Field saw the first World Series on artificial turf in 1970.*

Three Rivers Stadium
Pittsburgh (1970–2000)

In the late 1960s the Pittsburgh Pirates played ball in Forbes Field, considered small (capacity 35,000) and dilapidated by Pirates owners. Like most teams of the era, the Pirates went looking for a new ballpark. When the adjacent University of Pittsburgh came knocking on the door needing more room, it was enough to get the Pirates into a new home. But the transition wasn't an easy one. Ground breaking took place in April 1968, then construction hit one snag after another. Opening day was delayed in early 1970, then delayed again. Finally, on July 16, 1970, Three Rivers Stadium opened for business.

Remarkably similar to Riverfront Stadium, which opened just three weeks earlier and sat on the same Ohio River, Three Rivers Stadium was named for its vantage point at the intersection of the Allegheny, Monongahela, and Ohio rivers. Like Riverfront before it, this park sported dirt "patches," which the bases and the pitcher's mound peeked through. Other than that, it was artificial turf all the way. The outfield was symmetrical and, at 400 feet (122m) in center and 335 feet (102m) at the foul poles, was not even long or short enough to be interesting. Not surprisingly, this lack of character didn't help at the turnstiles. In 2000, the last year for Three Rivers Stadium, the Pirates pulled in a measly average of 21,591 fans per game.

Pittsburgh was looking to take the wrecking ball to Three Rivers Stadium for years. Only four years after a task force was set up to explore a new Pittsburgh stadium, the Pirates broke ground on a new old-style ballpark, which opened in 2001. Named after the financial services company that shelled out nearly $30 million for the naming rights, PNC Park was the first ballpark with a two-deck design to be built in the United States since Milwaukee's County Stadium was completed in 1953. With a little over 38,000 seats, the new park is one of the smallest in the majors, and looks to be a classy reward for all those Pirates fans who endured the years in Three Rivers Stadium, which was demolished on February 11, 2001.

Veterans Stadium
Philadelphia (1971–2003)

The last of the concrete-doughnut stadiums to come into play, "The Vet" was right at home in the multistadium complex in which it sat. Located right next to the First Union Center and the First Union Spectrum, Veterans Stadium is a large concrete tub among large concrete tubs, and scored a zero for external charm among many baseball fans. "The place looks trashy," remarks author Bob Wood in *Dodger Dogs to Fenway Franks: The Ultimate Guide to America's Top Baseball Parks.* Unfortunately, Wood's critique doesn't improve once he hands over his ticket. "Inside, stadium tackiness intensifies," he writes, noting the park's hideous color scheme.

Veterans Stadium replaced the venerable old Connie Mack Stadium, formerly known as Shibe Park. The first concrete-and-steel stadium in the majors, Shibe Park was constructed in less than a year, typical for the era. Having seen more than sixty years of baseball from both the Philadelphia A's and the Phillies, the old park was starting to show its age by the late '60s. It also had no parking and sat in a decaying neighborhood. So, in 1971, Philadelphia replaced cozy little Connie Mack Stadium with a two-level concrete behemoth that held more than 62,000 fans.

Philly ran into trouble from the start of the project, and cost overruns forced the city to get approval for a second bond issuance in 1967. But the project continued, and on April 4, 1971, a helicopter hovered over the new stadium to throw in the first pitch to Phillies catcher Mike Ryan. Since that time Philly's concrete doughnut has seen three World Series (one successful for the home team, in 1980) and two All-Star games. It also saw some neglect, and in 1994 the Phillies took over management of the yard from the city of Philadelphia.

As for baseball charm, you'll have to look elsewhere. The field was almost a carbon copy of Three Rivers and Riverfront stadiums: artificial turf with dirt patches at the bases and the pitcher's mound. One of the few distinguishing characteristics was a replica Liberty Bell that used to hang from center field, which was dinged by a Greg Luzinski home run in 1972.

ABOVE: *Later renamed Connie Mack Stadium, Philadelphia's Shibe Park was hailed as the crown jewel of ballparks when it opened in 1909.*

RIGHT: *Fans line up for tickets outside Shibe, home to the Philadelphia Athletics from 1909 to 1954 and the Philadelphia Phillies from 1938 to 1970.*

Unfortunately, the story is the same as it was at Riverfront and Three Rivers when it comes to long-term success. In its later years, attendance at Veterans Stadium was among the lowest in the majors, averaging only 20,486 per game in 2002 (although that number got a final-goodbye bump to 28,973 in 2003). As the Phillies got ready for a 2004 move to a sparkling new stadium, dubbed Citizens Bank Park, the old Vet got a final send-off. On September 28, 2003, over 58,000 fans gathered to witness the last game at Veterans Stadium, but not everyone was shedding tears. "Everybody's trying to make this like we should all be crying because they're going to tear down the Vet," hall-of-fame Phillie Mike Schmidt said. "It must not have much significance if they're going to blow it up, right?"

ABOVE: *A night game at Veterans Stadium, 1999.*

Olympic Stadium
Montreal (opened 1977)

For the city of Montreal, it seemed the best of plans. First, you acquire a National League expansion franchise with the provision that you will build a domed stadium to house your new team. Then you snag the 1976 Olympic games. You hire a Parisian architect to build an ultra-modern stadium that will house track and field for the '76 Games, and baseball thereafter. To top it all off, the ballpark will be the model for a new generation of retractable-roof parks, allowing open-air baseball in fair weather yet keeping out the Canadian frost on chillier nights. Sounds great, right? Well, two decades and $1 billion later, the Expos now find themselves with a broken-down ballpark and the lowest attendance in the major leagues.

The sad story goes like this: in a major coup for Canada, Major League Baseball awarded an expansion franchise to a group of Montreal businessmen in 1968, creating the first major league baseball team outside the United States. The city christened their new team the Expos after Montreal's "Expo '67" World's Fair, and chose for their home a cozy little municipal stadium called Jarry Park. With a capacity for only 3,000 fans, Jarry Park was quickly renovated, and by opening day of the 1969 season, its capacity was increased to over 28,000. It was nothing fancy, but it did the trick until a new stadium could be built.

Nicknamed the Big O, Olympic Stadium rose like a visitor from outer space in time to host the 1976 Olympic Games. And what an alien it was. Impressively flat with wide support arches flowing down its side, Olympic Stadium was the height of modernism. The structure featured a 556-foot (170m) leaning tower hovering over the stadium, bent auspiciously at a 45-degree angle. Taller than the Washington Monument and leaning nine times steeper than the Leaning Tower of Pisa, the Olympic Stadium tower was at the center of the state-of-the-art retractable-roof system. The tower stood unfinished from

LEFT: *Montreal's billion-dollar Olympic Stadium debuted a wonder of engineering and design, but it has had a hard time keeping its seats full.*

1976 to 1987, and was finally operational in 1989. The massive roof was constructed of more than 60,000 square feet (18,288sq m) of Kevlar, weighing in at a whopping 50 tons. Painted orange on the inside and silver on the exterior, the roof is covered with twenty-six white points that connect it with the tower. Unfortunately, the roof's function never caught up to its style, and many problems were encountered in its operation. It has now remained closed for many

seasons, and in January 1999 five people were injured when a panel of the roof gave way under the weight of wet snow.

Olympic Stadium was the first international ballpark. Both the Canadian and the American national anthems are played before every game, and messages on the scoreboard appear in both English and French. A statue of Jackie Robinson stands in the main entrance of Olympic Stadium, a tribute from the city where Robinson got his major league start in the Dodgers' farm system.

The stadium itself stands as a testament to the promises and disappointments of the modern ballpark era. Fluorescent artificial turf

ABOVE: *Originally built for the 1976 Olympics, Montreal's "Big O" seems more suited to track and field than to baseball.*

covers the field, looked down upon by 46,500 seats with views that are perhaps better suited to track and field than to baseball. All in all, Wrigley Field it ain't.

Through the 1970s, '80s, and '90s, Montreal has built an impressive organization that has been home to a parade of talented young players such as Rusty Staub, Andre Dawson, Tim Wallach, Henry Rodriguez, and Pedro Martinez, only to see them get bought off by deep-pocketed competitors. Without the revenue base to compete, the Expos have never been to the World Series in their entire history.

At the end of the twentieth century, the Expos and their spaceship stadium found themselves hanging on for dear life. Montreal has, by far, the lowest attendance numbers of any major league city, and in 2003, attracted only 812,045 fans for the *entire season*, an average of only 10,025 per game.

Like most teams saddled with outdated parks, Montreal has visions of a new ball yard. In June 1997, Expos owners even unveiled plans for a new, downtown baseball stadium with a retractable roof. But, not surprisingly, as well-heeled American cities clamor for professional sports franchises, Montreal finds itself close to losing the Expos. In November 2001, Major League owners voted to contract two franchises for the 2002 season, and Montreal was widely speculated to be a candidate. Those contractions were later delayed, but not before Jeffrey Loria, the owner of the Expos, sold the team back to the league. To add insult to injury, the Expos played twenty-two home games for the 2003 season in Puerto Rico. And with that, the Expos achieved a rare baseball milestone: the first team to start vacating their ballpark before they officially move out.

RIGHT: *Olympic Stadium's space-age retractable roof has remained closed for many seasons.*

CHAPTER 3

The Revival Era, 1990–present

While it's too early to call this period a golden age of baseball parks, by all indications it might just be one. During this time, more than fifteen new major league ballparks have been inaugurated, a trend that continues with new ballparks seemingly always in the works. There's no doubt that these years will have an enormous impact on what the game will look like in the twenty-first century and beyond. There are a slew of reasons why the old parks got the bulldozer, and a lot of them boil down to money and luxury-box revenue. But look deeper, and the real reason lies with the folks in the seats.

OPPOSITE: *The mile-high view from the upper decks of Denver's Coors Field.*

Cozy new stadiums like Jacobs Field in Cleveland have brought back the intimate ballpark experience.

Today, as it did in the years immediately after World War II, baseball once again finds itself mirroring society. When postwar Americans abandoned the cities for the suburbs and hopped off trolleys and into autos, baseball built a generation of monolithic coliseums with sprawling parking lots on the outskirts of town. But as a rejuvenation of American cities began in the 1980s, and the country entered a period of prolonged economic prosperity, people soon got tired of the faceless 'burbs. Style looked backward and anything old became hip, as the

Volkswagen Bug made a comeback and Austin Powers swept the United States. Baseball got wise, and saw that its future was in its past.

Toss on your cap and march into one of the new ballparks, and you're struck with a wonderful contradiction. First, many of these ballparks have gone out of their way to adopt the charm of yesteryear's classic parks. The majestic spread of a real grass field is a given, and small baseball-only configurations are the rule of the day. On the other hand, today's new field of dreams is a technological marvel, with big bucks spent

on groundskeeping technology and space-age retractable roofs. While the architects of the '60s and '70s stadiums could be shot for some of the choices they made (we're all still scratching our heads over Astroturf), at least they taught us what *not* to do. Rest assured, today's ballpark builder has learned from past mistakes.

The results are a team of rookie parks that look like Hall of Fame material. Pacific Bell Park, sandwiched in a corner of San Francisco's South of Market district, is a cozy little park with a classic brick exterior that hearkens back to Ebbets Field. Quirky little Jacobs Field in Cleveland not only revitalized a downtown neighborhood, but vaulted the also-ran Indians

into perennial pennant threats. And SAFECO Field gave Mariners fans a classic baseball-friendly replacement for the massive Kingdome, while its "umbrella"-style roof combines an open-air vibe with protection from Seattle's inevitable downpours.

There's no guarantee that the new sandlots of today will be the classics of tomorrow. In twenty years we may look back at today's technological marvels and think, "Retractable roofs, what were we thinking?" But judging by the mobs of fans decked out in Orioles jackets streaming into Camden Yards, chances are these new ballparks are a pretty good bet.

The intimate confines of Atlanta's new Turner Field in the foreground contrast sharply with the coldness of Atlanta–Fulton County Stadium in the background.

Oriole Park at Camden Yards

Baltimore (opened 1992)

By the late 1980s baseball parks were in a pretty sad state of affairs. Many of the old baseball-only parks had been swapped for concrete multi-purpose stadiums (as in Pittsburgh, Cincinnati, and Philadelphia) and of the ones that remained, quite a few were getting ready for the wrecking ball (like Tiger Stadium in Detroit and Comiskey Park in Chicago). From an architectural and historical perspective, ballparks were clearly at a crossroads. Many observers of parks clearly asked, "What's next?"

To answer the question, the city of Baltimore stepped up to the plate, and in the process changed the course of ballparks forever. It can be said that no single structure has more greatly affected the history of baseball parks than Oriole Park at Camden Yards. As a throwback to the cozy, intimate confines of yesteryear, Camden Yards ushered in a new era of retro ball yards. With a classic brick facade, intimate seating, and a century-old warehouse looming just beyond center field, Camden Yards has inspired a new generation of parks in almost a dozen cities.

Although Camden Yards has become a symbol of the modern ballpark, its birth arose more out of survival than of trailblazing. Having already lost the football Colts, Baltimore was determined to hang on to their beloved Orioles. Even though the cavernous Memorial Stadium was still in acceptable condition and pulling in around 30,000 fans a game, the city of Baltimore looked for a new park to keep the Orioles in town. The effort got a big boost when the baseball-minded William Donald Schaefer, former mayor of Baltimore, became governor of Maryland and made a new Oriole park a priority. Fortunately, the Orioles simultaneously got a new owner in New York banker Eli Jacobs, a fan of architecture. Together, they pushed for and got a new field.

Construction of Camden Yards began on June 28, 1989. It would be finished in thirty-three months, but before the first ball was thrown out, a name had to be decided on. Schaefer wanted to call the confines Camden Yards after a nineteenth-century Baltimore railway station. Jacobs opted for Oriole Park after the International League park that stood in Baltimore until the '40s. A compromise strung the two names together, and on April 6, 1992, Oriole Park at Camden Yards debuted, with a mouthful of a name now generally truncated to "Camden Yards."

The dimensions of Camden Yards show the influence of the classic parks. Like the late

BELOW: *Cal Ripken, Jr. takes the last at-bat of his career at Camden Yards in Baltimore on October 6, 2001.*

OPPOSITE: *Baltimore's Camden Yards is widely credited with the return of the intimate ballpark.*

Ebbets Field in Brooklyn, Camden Yards features an asymmetrical outfield, measuring 410 feet (125m) at deepest left-center, 333 feet (101m) in left, and 318 feet (97m) in right. The hitter-friendly dimensions of right field are frustrated by a 25-foot (7.5m) fence, which sports a digital "game in progress" scoreboard. A natural grass surface and steel trusses (rather than concrete) give Camden Yards a wonderfully classic baseball feel. The scoreboard in center field is topped with a vintage-look clock, surrounded by the letters THE SUN, an ad for the local Baltimore newspaper whose H and E light up as a hit/error indicator.

Nothing gives this park a more metropolitan feel than the immense brick B&O warehouse looming just beyond the right-field wall. Built between 1889 and 1905, the B&O is the largest building on the East Coast, measuring 1,116 feet (340m) long. Today the eight-story brick landmark houses the ballpark's operations and kitchen facilities, as well as the Orioles team office. More than a neighboring building, it is actually part of the game, since the right-field lights hang from the warehouse's roof. It also played a part in a historic countdown in 1995. During that memorable season, numbers soaring 10 feet (3m) high hung from the B&O as Cal

Ripken marched toward Lou Gehrig's longstanding record of 2,131 consecutive games played.

Camden Yards sports great sight lines and fantastic seating. But a couple of the seats stand out among the rest. A red seat in left field marks the spot where Cal Ripken landed his 278th homer on July 15, 1993, surpassing Ernie Banks for most home runs hit by a shortstop. And in the right-field bleachers, look for a special seat that marks the landing of Eddie Murray's 500th home run, which he dinged on September 6, 1996, to become only the fifteenth player to reach the 500 club.

When most fans think of Babe Ruth they think of New York, and perhaps Boston. But Camden Yards is steeped in Ruth history. Ruth started his career with the minor league Orioles, who signed him for a paltry $600 in 1914. Unfortunately, the struggling Orioles had to sell the Babe, who went to the Red Sox for five seasons before becoming a legendary Yankee. The birthplace of the Bambino is just blocks away, and today a 9-foot (2.7m) bronze statue of Ruth sits at the entrance near the north end of the warehouse. Center field at Camden Yards is now a patch of majestic grass, but it was once the site of the saloon owned by Ruth's father.

ABOVE: *Ticket to the 1958 All-Star game held at Memorial Stadium, home of the Orioles from 1954 to 1991.* **BELOW:** *The Orioles insignia adorns a gate that first swung open on April 6, 1992.* **OPPOSITE:** *Camden Yards, where every seat is in on the action.*

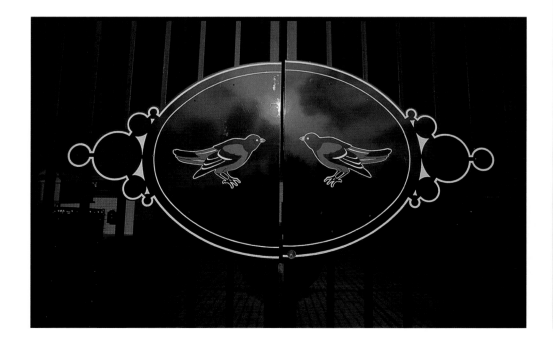

Jacobs Field
Cleveland (opened 1994)

Cleveland's Jacobs Field is one of the most perfect ballparks in baseball. After spending many long years in the cold, cavernous Cleveland Stadium (dubbed "The Mistake by the Lake"), the Indians deserve Jacobs Field. So dramatic was the move that writer Ed Sherman called the switch "like moving from Siberia to Maui."

Along with Camden Yards in Baltimore, Jacobs Field has become synonymous with the return of open-air, natural-grass ballparks. Seating just over 43,000, Jacobs Field is a snug little park located right in the heart of Cleveland. No doubt about it, this joint was designed with the fan in mind. Seats are generous in width and angled toward the playing field. With the Cleveland skyline looming in the background, the park sports a quirky, asymmetrical playing field and natural-grass playing surface.

Left field ends at a 19–foot (5.8m) "mini monster" (nicknamed in deference to the infamous Green Monster at Boston's Fenway Park),

ABOVE: *Collectible Indians scorecard.* **BELOW:** *The return to natural-grass fields is a hallmark of today's retro ballparks.* **LEFT:** *Once a rookie in the ranks of ballparks, Jacobs Field is now considered one of the granddaddies of revival ballparks.*

complete with game-in-progress scoreboard. In a throwback to old parks, the scoreboard in left field is plastered with advertisements.

It's no coincidence that as soon as the Indians took up residence in Jacobs Field they shot to the top of the Central Division of the American League—increased revenue from all those sold-out games bought quality players. Before the construction of Jacobs Field, the Indians hadn't seen a pennant since 1954. In the new yard, the boys from Cleveland have been to the fall classic twice, in 1995 and 1997.

In Jacobs Field, almost everything is a mixture of old charm and modern reality. Even the name is a hybrid of old and new. In the early part of the twentieth century, ballparks were named after powerful owners, like Wrigley Field, Comiskey Park, and Ebbets Field. Nowadays the corporation reigns supreme, and even the name above the turnstile isn't immune to corporate money. Witness the large sums paid just for the naming rights to SBC Park, SAFECO Field, Coors Field, and Comerica Park. Jacobs Field gets its moniker from Richard Jacobs, the

Indians owner who fought so hard to keep baseball in Cleveland. But it wasn't all sentimental: Jacobs also forked over $13 million for the naming rights.

Of course, this is twenty-first century baseball, and fan comfort notwithstanding, the real benchmark of ballpark performance is at the ticket booth. In this respect, the Indians knocked it out of the park, at least at first. In 1996, before a single inning had been played, the Indians sold out the entire season, an unprecedented feat made more amazing by the fact that they had repeat preseason sellouts in 1997, 1998, and 1999. The average attendance at Jacobs Field in 1998 was more than 42,000—their highest ever. As late as 2001, Cleveland was still in the top five in major league attendance, pulling in almost 40,000 fans per game. But by 2003, as a result of a mediocre team (over 90 losses that year), the number of bodies per game had dwindled to 21,358. Moving forward, the Indians will have to field a competitive team to get fans out to this awesome sandlot.

BELOW: *Jacobs Field opened in Cleveland in 1994, and was one of a series of new retro ballparks that revolutionized major league parks and their economics.*

OPPOSITE: *The return to natural-grass fields is a hallmark of today's retro ballparks.*

RIGHT: *Arlington Stadium, home to the Texas Rangers from 1972 to 1993, was built in a natural bowl with the playing surface forty feet below the area around it.*

Ballpark in Arlington

Arlington, Texas (opened 1994)

The Ballpark in Arlington is part modern stadium, part retro ballpark, and part amusement park. It went up in just twenty-three months at a cost of $191 million, and saw its first game on April 1, 1994. This modern gem is located right next to Six Flags Over Texas, a 200-acre (80ha) amusement park.

The Ballpark in Arlington replaced Arlington Stadium, the field which had been the home of the Texas Rangers for twenty-two years. Originally named Turnpike Stadium, Arlington Stadium housed a number of minor league teams from Dallas and Fort Worth in its cozy 10,000-seat confines. When the Washington Senators decided to move to Texas for the 1972 season, the park changed its name and tripled in capacity to welcome its new major league team. But after two decades, the old stadium had outlived its usefulness, and a new stadium was planned for the 1994 season.

The new Ballpark in Arlington is a jewel of a ballpark, with a retro red granite and brick exterior. Two large brick towers welcome visitors, and the archway features thirty-five steer heads and twenty-one lone stars cast out of stone. A brick "Walk of Fame" rings the entire perimeter of the ballpark, and tells the story of the Texas Rangers from their birth in 1971.

One thing's for sure: this ain't your grandfather's ballpark. Inside the amenities really begin. The Ballpark in Arlington features the Legends of the Game Baseball Museum, a 17,000-square-foot (5181sq m) exhibit with a 225-seat theater; a picnic area just beyond center field, an art gallery beyond that, and a children's learning center. In case that wasn't enough, they decided to create a 12-acre (4.8ha) lake right next door.

Not to be lost among the amenities is an actual baseball park, which sports some quirky asymmetrical outfield dimensions. One of the unique features of the park is a two-tiered home run porch in right field, modeled after the design made famous at Detroit's Tiger Stadium—but this one is tailored for Texas weather, with ceiling fans whirring away overhead.

LEFT: *The ballpark in Arlington: part retro ballpark, part modern stadium, and part amusement park.*

OPPOSITE TOP: *The brick facades of today's ballparks hearken back to the days of Ebbets Field and other classic sandlots.*

LEFT: *Texas Ranger catcher Ivan Rodriguez goes over the rail fielding a foul ball in the Ballpark in Arlington in 1998.*

BELOW: *The Ballpark in Arlington features a two-tiered right-field "porch" reminiscent of the late Tiger Stadium in Detroit.*

Coors Field

Denver (opened 1995)

Along with Camden Yards and Jacobs Field, Coors Field is one of the "crown jewel" baseball yards credited with the revival of the old-time ballpark. This majestic sandlot sits in a previously industrial section of downtown Denver known as "LoDo." One expansion team and $215 million later, the area has now become a mecca for baseball fans, and no tour of baseball parks would be complete without some time at Coors Field.

Coors Field is an almost perfect mix of old and new. The ballpark itself sits on the site of Denver's first railroad station, Denver Pacific Depot, and its magnificent architecture is right at home in the neighborhood. The exterior is hand-laid brick, and the main entrance is topped by an old-fashioned clock tower. The words COORS FIELD spelled out in shiny silver letters greet the visitor upon entry. And even though the diamond is kept immaculately snow-free by an advanced heating system below the surface, it is still looked upon by a manual scoreboard in right field.

Coors Field has been known as a hitter's park from the day it opened. The foul territory at Coors Field is among the smallest in baseball, with about 56 feet (17m) between home plate and the first row—good for fans trying to get close to the game, bad for pitchers looking for

RIGHT: The majestic entrance to Coors Field, considered one of the most intimate professional ballparks in the country.
BELOW: A Colorado Rockies pennant.

the quick foul out. With outfield corners at 420 and 424 feet (128 and 28.6m), you'd think this park would be a hurler's dream. Think again.

The biggest foe a pitcher has in Denver is the altitude. In research on ballparks and home runs, mathematician Howard Penn of the United States Naval Academy found that altitude far outweighs field dimensions when determining home-run success, and he estimated that a baseball travels 10 percent farther in Coors Field than in any other major-league park. Asked to compare the number of home runs hit by a team playing at home with the number hit by the same team on the road, Penn noted, "Coors Field was way out of line" with other parks. And in case you're not sure how high up this park is, check out the upper deck. Six rows from the top, you'll find a row of purple seats marking the precise mile-high point, 5,280 feet (1609m) above sea level.

In terms of charm, amenities, and excitement, Coors Field is one of the best in the majors, and it's also one of the largest of the revival parks. The Rockies' stadium was originally designed to seat 43,800, but in their inaugural season in 1993, this expansion team packed Mile High Stadium, setting a major league single-season attendance record of 4,483,350. This sent the owners scurrying back to the drawing board to bring Coors Field up to its current capacity of over 50,000. While Coors Field was consistently a top draw among the majors during its first few years, the Rockies uninspiring play on the field in the late '90s and early '00s led to dwindling numbers. Let's hope that in the future there's a more solid team in Colorado to draw fans to this sparkler of a ballpark.

LEFT: *The view from the outfield at Denver's Coors Field. Today's new ballparks are not only popular with fans, but players too.*

Bank One Ballpark
Phoenix (opened 1998)

When Bank One Ballpark opened its doors on March 31, 1998, there was no denying that ballparks had entered a whole new era. Nicknamed BOB and costing a whopping $356 million to build, this glitzy oasis shocked baseball purists, who saw its endless parade of amusements as a distraction from the grand old game. But whether you like it or not, there's no denying that Bank One Ballpark is a window into the future of ballparks. Get used to it.

From the outside, it's difficult to tell if Bank One Ballpark is a retro-style ballpark or a warehouse. With an exterior of red brick and green structural steel, it looks like a mixture of both. The most distinctive feature of Bank One is a massive retractable roof that helps shield fans from the brutal Arizona heat. The ballpark's roof is comprised of nine million pounds (4.1 million kg) of steel, and can be opened in less than five minutes by a pair of 200–horsepower motors. The unique roof allows for what is called "sun tracking," which involves adjusting the roof for maximum sun on the field and maximum shade on the seats. The park also sports a massive air-conditioning system, which can bring the temperature down by 30°F (about 18°C) in just three hours.

As for the amenities, it's difficult to know where to start. Within its humble walls, Bank One Ballpark features a two-story baseball museum and a massive multimedia baseball exhibit with 130 monitors. For those who are hungry, the park has an incredible quarter mile (.4km) of concession stands, as well as a number of specialty stands, including a farmer's market. No one goes thirsty here, with an on-site microbrewery and two 6,000-square-foot (1829m²) beer gardens. But the most extravagant amenity of all is the Sun Pool Party Pavilion, located a few feet from the action beyond the wall in right-center field. Up to thirty-five people can book the pavilion and field homers from the pool; the only thing between them and the fielders is a see-through home run wall.

Seating was a major priority when designing BOB, and more than 80 percent of the seats are inside the foul poles. Seats are extra wide, and there's a cup holder at every seat. And as baseball enters an era of polarity, where the cheap

seats are really cheap and the swanky boxes cost a fortune, this ballpark leads the way. For those on a budget (and with good hiking shoes), the ultra-steep upper-level seats are dirt cheap. At the other end of the spectrum, the well-heeled get pampered in the Diamond Level, with access to a swanky private club that is the equal of anything in Hollywood.

But considering all the money and attention put into this high-tech field, a singular symbol of baseball simplicity somehow found its way into the design. In a rare throwback to yes-teryear, Bank One Ballpark sports a dirt path between the pitcher's mound and home plate, a charming feature not seen in a major league park in decades.

ABOVE: *BOB's high-tech retractable roof is comprised of nine million pounds of steel.*
RIGHT: *The Diamondbacks are a team that spares no expense on their ballpark or on their star players, like the pricey Randy Johnson.*

SAFECO Field
Seattle (opened 1999)

Let it not be said that the road to revival is cheap. In 1997, after spending twenty years playing on the Astroturf of the football-friendly Kingdome, the Seattle Mariners began a journey toward a new state-of-the-art ballpark. The fare for the road trip: a whopping $517 million. With a tab final for the stadium and surrounding projects costing $100 million above original estimates, SAFECO Field now stands as the most expensive American baseball stadium project of the twentieth century.

SAFECO Field is one of the most technologically advanced ballparks in the country. Located a stone's throw from the Kingdome in downtown Seattle, the Mariners' new ballpark is a hybrid of the best of the old ballparks and state-of-the-art technology. The ballpark holds a baseball-friendly 47,000 people, and features a real grass field. But to see the true innovations made at SAFECO, you have to look literally high and low.

SAFECO Field is one of a new generation of retractable-roof ball fields. Given Seattle's

perennially soggy climate, this is understandable. But what makes this park unique is its retractable "umbrella"-style roof. While most stadiums with retractable roofs close the lid as tight as a mayonnaise jar, SAFECO's roof simply covers the stadium. This allows protection from the elements, yet still provides an open-air feeling. The roof is made of three panels that span railroad tracks, which can be rolled closed in 10–20 minutes, even when games are in progress. The massive roof weighs in at about 11,000 tons and contains enough steel to build a fifty-five-story skyscraper.

SAFECO has a few clever tricks to offer under foot, as well. There used to be a day when growing a grass playing field meant tossing some seed on the ground and watering it. But SAFECO Field has taken the art of groundskeeping to new heights, or more appropriately, depths. Below the surface at SAFECO Field lies one of the most complicated infrastructures of any field. More than 20 miles (32km) of one-inch (2.54cm) plastic hose is snaked below the playing surface. Warm water circulating through the

hoses can warm the playing surface to 50–65°F (10–18°C), which compensates for lack of sunlight and helps fool the grass out of dormancy about three months early in the spring.

But whatever the expense or science that's gone into this yard, the results have sure pleased the fans, who come to this park in droves. SAFECO Field consistently ranks among the top draws in the majors. In 2003, the park had an average game attendance of 40,351, which is not only impressive, but catapults this greenhorn up there with the veterans. The only park to pull in more people per game that year: New York's Yankee Stadium.

OPPOSITE: *Fireworks light up the cap of the Kingdome, the Mariner's domed home until 1999.* **BELOW:** *Seattle Mariner pitcher Jamie Moyer delivers the first pitch at Seattle's SAFECO Field on opening day, July 15, 1999.*

The umbrella-style retractable roof at SAFECO Field keeps out the rain while still providing an open air feeling.

Minute Maid Park
Houston (opened 2000)

After thirty-one years of slugging it out in the Astrodome, in 1996 the Houston Astros had had enough of their space-age ballpark. With other cities using revenue from swanky new ballparks to build championship teams, the Astros jumped on the new-stadium bandwagon. After the Houston Oilers left for Tennessee, Houston realized that the threat of sports teams leaving town was more than idle, and the momentum for a new ballpark picked up steam.

Looking to duplicate the successes in Baltimore and Cleveland, Astros owner Drayton McLane, Jr., pushed to build a downtown ballpark, reversing the suburban migration of ballparks that started in the 1960s. In 1995 McLane came close to selling the team to Virginia businessmen who wanted a ball team for suburban Washington, D.C. But in late 1996 the voters of Harris County approved a new ballpark. Ground breaking on the new park, which was to be called the Ballpark at Union Station, occurred on October 30, 1997.

BELOW: *An aerial view of Houston's Enron field during the construction process.*
OPPOSITE: *Minute Maid Park was designed to keep out the humid Texas weather.*

THE REVIVAL ERA, 1990—PRESENT

BELOW: *Houston Astros pitcher Octavio Dotel throws the first pitch in Minute Maid Park (then Enron Field) on opening day, April 7, 2000.*
OPPOSITE: *Minute Maid Park in Houston features an immense steel retractable roof weighing over 7,600 metric tons.*

An intimate stadium holding almost 41,000 fans, the stadium sports a natural-surface playing field and a classic brick facade. Playing summer ball in Houston can be a humid affair, but many fans found the perennially air-conditioned Astrodome to be too artificial a substitute. Today's Astros look to have it both ways with a massive, state-of-the-art retractable roof allowing an open-air baseball field on days that permit it. Built to withstand a hurricane, the roof will open and close in twelve minutes, and do so efficiently. The cost of the roof is estimated at $65 million, with energy costs estimated at just $5 per usage. The roof is expected to roll open about eighty times a year, traveling 14.6 miles (23km)

over its transport tracks annually. Estimated life expectancy: 50 years or 730 miles (1175km).

The Astros' new ballpark is more than a great new home for America's pastime; it's insurance against the Astros skipping town, as they've signed a thirty-year lease on the new yard. In April 1999, the Astros penned a naming rights deal with the infamous Enron, an arrangement that gave this field its initial moniker of "Enron Field." When Enron went down in well-publicized flames in 2002, the team bought back the naming rights and gave this yard the temporary name of "Astros Field" until they struck a new naming deal with Coca-Cola later that year.

SBC Park
San Francisco (opened 2000)

Few new ballparks have been as big of a hit as SBC Park. If you're looking for old-time charm, updated amenities, and excellence on the field, no place in the majors has got the goods like this park by the bay.

After spending more than thirty years in Candlestick Park, the San Francisco Giants by 1996 were in a tough way. The team was losing money, and fans were universally rejecting their frigid wind tunnel of a ballpark. Just three years earlier, things had looked much rosier. Led by Safeway chairman and CEO Peter Magowan, a group of local businesspeople had bought the club and saved it from an exodus to Florida. They scooped up superstar free agent Barry Bonds, and built a solid team that came within one game of winning the 1993 division title. Not only that, it looked like they had enough momentum to get a new stadium built in the city of San Francisco, which most observers agreed was the key to the Giants' long-term viability.

But getting a new park was no easy task. San Francisco voters rejected funding for a new stadium four times, demonstrating a brand of shallow-pocketed thrift the *Wall Street Journal* later called "voter fatigue." Giants owners decided to try another route. In December 1995 the team unveiled plans for a nice little downtown park, located in San Francisco's South of Market district. This little gem of a ballpark was everything Candlestick Park wasn't: small and cozy, with classic architectural features and, most of all, better weather. But its best feature was the financial cost to the city. Total amount of public money needed for direct construction: $0.

The Giants envisioned paying for their ballpark by selling most parts of it, including the name itself. In addition, the team would market an aggressive number of "charter seat licenses," basically the right to buy season tickets. Overall the plan was for corporations and season-ticket holders—not the general public—to carry the

RIGHT: *At SBC Park, the short right field fence with McCovey Cove just beyond has made for many soggy four-baggers.* **ABOVE:** *One of the first things to go up in San Francisco's new park was home plate.*

financial load. It was a formula for the '90s, and in March 1996 voters took the bait, approving the construction of the first privately funded ballpark since Dodger Stadium in 1962.

Everything about this park is designed to be a mix of new and old. The Giants' new ballpark is squeezed into a 13-acre (5.2ha) site and seats just over 41,000. Designed by HOK Sport, the same firm responsible for Camden Yards and Jacobs Field, SBC Park sports a classic brick facade that fits in perfectly with the warehouses of this once-industrial part of the city. The small amount of foul territory creates intimate seating reminiscent of Ebbets Field, and the seats themselves are extra wide and angled toward home plate.

SBC Park is tucked right up against San Francisco Bay and, like many of its predecessors, its irregular dimensions are a result of being squeezed into an urban neighborhood. In this park, the water isn't just a spectator, it plays backup to the right fielder. With the right field fence only 307 feet (94m) from home plate, dingers regularly land in a tiny inlet affectionately named McCovey Cove after Giants slugger Willie McCovey. This tradition of soggy four-baggers started when Barry Bonds hit the park's first home run into the water on May 1, 2000.

Every inch of SBC Park is designed with reverence for the past, an impression that greets the visitor from the front door. The entire entrance to the park on Third and King Streets is a tribute to Willie Mays, one of the greatest players ever to wear a Giants uniform. A statue of Mays in the middle of a monster swing stands at the entrance to the park, surrounded by twenty-four palm trees in honor of the number the "Say Hey Kid" wore as a Giant. Even the park's mailing address, 24 Willie Mays Plaza, honors the slugger.

Without a doubt, the biggest change from Candlestick Park to SBC Park is the weather. The Giant's old park was famous for its hurricane gusts that made playing the outfield a high-wire act. For fans, a day at Candlestick was a frigid affair, and wool mittens were standard baseball attire. So it's not surprising that the designers of SBC Park worked overtime to shield players and fans from the hearty San Francisco winds. By all accounts, they succeeded beautifully. SBC Park is located in one of the sunniest parts of the city, and the ballpark was specifically designed to reduce wind. The result: while the

The San Francisco Giants battle the Los Angeles Dodgers on opening day at SBC Park, April 11, 2000.

wind may be howling around the Willie Mays statue on Third Street, the air at home plate won't move a peanut wrapper. In fact, the design is so successful that Giants coach Sonny Jackson thinks the team may lose home field advantage. "The only bad thing about it is people are going to enjoy coming here to play," Jackson said in 1999. "Now, [at Candlestick Park] people hated coming here and playing because of the wind. That's been to our advantage."

But let's face it, a major part of this field's allure is the stellar baseball being played on it. In the first four years of play in SBC Park, the Giants progressed to the postseason three times, reaching the World Series in 2002. And if you want to talk about the Giants' on-field dominance since relocating to SBC Park, just say two words: Barry Bonds. This future hall-of-famer has been breaking records like crazy since moving into these cozy confines. During his first four years in the Giants' new park, Bonds set records for the most home runs in a season, the most walks in a season, and the best on-base percentage; nabbed two National League MVP Awards; and hit his 600th home run in 2003. Simply awesome.

Put everything together, and you've got a park fans just can't stay away from. Outside of Boston's Fenway Park, no ball yard is more consistently full than SBC Park, which brought in over 3,000,000 fans in 2003 for the fourth consecutive year. And who can blame them? SBC Park is everything baseball should be, both on and off the field.

ABOVE: *Pacific Bell Park under construction on the edge of San Francisco Bay in June 1999.*

Comerica Park

Detroit
(opened 2000)

Never let it be said that a new ballpark is the complete answer to a baseball town's problems. Just ask Detroit. In the course of a couple of years at the dawn of the twenty-first century, this baseball hotbed saw the abandonment of a venerable sandlot, the construction of a shining new ball field, plummeting attendance, and one of the losingest teams in baseball history.

Rewind to the 1990s. Detroit decides to ditch historic Tiger Stadium and build a revival park as part of a downtown revitalization project. Note to baseball cities everywhere: never underestimate the fans' love of historic stadiums (especially if the stadium is eighty-five years old, as Tiger Stadium was in 1997). What followed was the precise opposite of a smooth transition to a new ballpark. After it was announced that Tiger Stadium would get the wrecking ball, fans revolted, and brought a lawsuit that went all the way to the Michigan Supreme Court. But the Tigers organization got its way, and finally broke ground on their new ballpark on October 29, 1997. In 2000, Detroit's new baseball stadium—named Comerica Park after the financial services company that had ponied up millions for the naming rights—witnessed the Tigers take on the Mariners on opening day.

And what a ballpark it was, as different from blue-collar Tiger Stadium as wieners are from tofu dogs. Comerica Park mingles baseball with a dizzying assortment of entertainment, including a carousel, a ferris wheel, and 70,000 square feet (6503m²) of retail space. Also included is a mammoth water feature in center field that can be choreographed to music. Surrounding the fun is an old-fashioned brick-and-steel stadium,

albeit with two sixty-foot (18.3m) baseball bats and a massive tiger statue guarding the entrance.

With a capacity of a little over 40,000, Comerica Park does away with upper-deck seats in the outfield and trades them for an unimpeded view of the Detroit skyline. But if distant vistas are what you're looking for, peer out at this park's fences from behind home plate. The massive dimensions of this field have proven to be a hitter's nightmare: 420 feet (128m) to the center-field wall, and 365 (111.3m) to right-center. "It was tough on [hitters], and understandably so," Tigers pitcher Steve Sparks told the Detroit Free Press in 2002. "They would hit a ball that may put us ahead, and time after time they got kind of cheated." In 2002, in an effort to drum up offense, the Tigers moved the left field fence closer by 20 feet (6m). But this hardly changed things. "Comerica Park will still be a pitchers' park," said Tigers President and General Manager Dave Dombrowski.

But for all the luster, the gleam coming from Comerica Park may actually be the reflection off the empty seats. Initiating a new trend of "build it, and they will come…for a year or so," the Tigers have seen attendance numbers plummet each year the new park has been open. From 2001 to 2003, the average attendance at Comerica Park dropped from 24,016 to a little over 17,000. In 2003, the average game at the Tigers' stadium was only 43 percent full, about half the numbers enjoyed by parks of similar vintage in San Francisco and Seattle.

True, many a Detroit fan may be pining away for old Tiger Stadium. But many of the empty chairs at Comerica Park may have less to do with the field than with the players on it. Starting with a dismal 79–83 in the stadium's inaugural 2000 season, the Tigers continued to do badly in 2001 and 2002. But nothing compared to the astonishingly lousy record the team put up in 2003. The Tigers just barely avoided the 1962 New York Mets' record for most losses in a season by winning their last game of the season, against the Minnesota Twins, on September 28, 2003. A mere 18,959 fans stopped by Comerica Park that day to witness the Tigers end their season at a near-historic 43–119.

For all the high-tech amenities and game-day giveaways, ballparks are still all about the game of baseball, and no one has learned that lesson better than the Detroit Tigers. "Comerica Park is a beautiful ballpark, but it doesn't bring people to the park by itself," Dave Dombrowski said to the Associated Press in 2002. "You have to have the team to draw people back….The ballpark is a big part of the foundation, but it's not the total solution."

Miller Park
Milwaukee
(opened 2001)

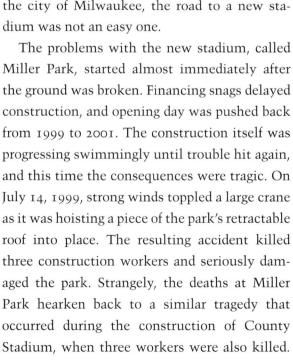

ABOVE: *A 1957 World Series ticket featuring the Milwaukee Braves, the only Wisconsin team ever to win the fall classic.* **RIGHT:** *County Stadium, the home of the Brewers until Miller Park is complete, has the unique distinction of being the only stadium with a beer keg in center field.*

For twenty-seven years, the Milwaukee Brewers played ball in County Stadium, a bland municipal ballpark as nondescript as its name. In many ways, County Stadium was as much of a hand-me-down as the team itself. The Brewers rose out of the ashes of the Seattle Pilots, an expansion franchise that lasted a single season before a group of Wisconsin businessmen brought the team to Milwaukee in 1970. To house their new team, the owners put County Stadium back in commission. (The yard was formerly the home of the Milwaukee Braves from 1953 to 1965, when they left town for Atlanta.) By 1999, the Brewers had almost three decades in County Stadium, and many said that a new ballpark was long overdue. But unfortunately for the Brewers and the city of Milwaukee, the road to a new stadium was not an easy one.

The problems with the new stadium, called Miller Park, started almost immediately after the ground was broken. Financing snags delayed construction, and opening day was pushed back from 1999 to 2001. The construction itself was progressing swimmingly until trouble hit again, and this time the consequences were tragic. On July 14, 1999, strong winds toppled a large crane as it was hoisting a piece of the park's retractable roof into place. The resulting accident killed three construction workers and seriously damaged the park. Strangely, the deaths at Miller Park hearken back to a similar tragedy that occurred during the construction of County Stadium, when three workers were also killed.

However, the work at Miller Park continued, and finally on April 6, 2001, Milwaukee's new yard saw its first regular season game.

The Brewers' new park stands in stark contrast to the antiquated tin-can look of County Stadium. Miller Park is downright gigantic inside, and robotic metal and machinery abound. Taken together with its retro brick exterior, it's as if someone tossed a batting glove into the gears of a baseball time machine. Miller Park features a towering, arched retractable-roof system, which has caused even more problems for the stadium. In the 2002 off-season, the Brewers not only had to make repairs to the roof's pivot system, but had to patch embarrassing leaks in the roof as well.

Few modern ballparks attempt to court their not-so-well-heeled patrons like Miller Park does. Here, you can literally get a seat for a buck, but there's a catch. Because of the massive workings of the retractable roof, some 200 to 300 seats have obstructed views. Dubbed "Uecker

seats" after radio broadcaster and baseball fun-nyman Bob Uecker, they sell for $1 on the day of the game.

But even dollar tickets can't draw fans to see underachievers like the Brewers. The boys from Milwaukee lost ninety or more games in each of their first three seasons at Miller Park, finish-ing dead last in 2002 and 2003. As a result, Milwaukee's new confines were little more than half-full on an average day in 2003, with just over 20,000 fans in the stands.

OPPOSITE: *The construction of Miller Park, which was delayed due to a tragic accident that killed three workers, looms large over County Stadium.* **NEXT PAGE:** *A rare sight in Milwaukee: a packed house at Miller Park on opening day, April 6, 2001. Attendance at the park has declined steadily ever since.*

BELOW: *Opening Day at PNC Park on April 9, 2000, with the majestic Pittsburgh skyline playing center field.*

OPPOSITE: *PNC Park, one of the smallest in the majors, was the first two-tier ball-park to be built in the United States since the 1950s.*

PNC Park

Pittsburgh
(opened 2001)

PNC Park stands in stark contrast to Three Rivers Stadium, the enormous mixed-use stadium the Pirates called home from 1970 to 1999. That concrete and AstroTurf mausoleum had a sizable 47,000-fan capacity. PNC Park reverses all that with a capacity of only 38,365, making it the second smallest ballpark in the majors (only Boston's Fenway Park is smaller). If cozy is what you like in a ballpark, this little field on the Allegheny River is for you. Opened in 2001, it is the first double-decker ballpark to be built in the United States since Milwaukee's County Stadium in 1953. And keep your glove handy— the highest seat is just 88 feet (26.8m) from the field.

The right and left field foul poles at PNC are only 320 and 325 feet (97.5 and 99m) respectively, which makes the park a delight for pull hitters. But the irregular field balloons to 410 feet (125m) deep at a nook located just left of

center field, 399 feet (121.6m) to center field, and 375 feet (114.3m) down the power alley. In honor of legendary Pirates right fielder Roberto Clemente, #21, the outfield wall rises up to 21 feet (6.4m) behind right field.

In addition to a classic brick-wall-and-steel-beam motif, PNC Park sports one of the most beautiful views in all of baseball, a spectacular panoramic of the Pittsburgh skyline. In fact, PNC Park is so well designed that ESPN Sports gave it the top rating among all major league stadiums. As ESPN.com's Eric Neel wrote in his Page 2 column in 2003, PNC Park is a "perfect blend of location, history, design, comfort and baseball. It's as if the House That Ruth Built had first been designed by Frank Lloyd Wright and then run past Ray Kinsella for final approval."

Unfortunately, while Pittsburgh's new park gets a golden glove when it comes to style, the park is all thumbs when it comes to attendance. Everything looked good for PNC Park back in 2001. During that inaugural season, the Pirates' new ballpark was pulling in an average

of 30,742 fans per game, over 80 percent of its capacity. But what a difference a couple of years make: in 2003, that number had gone down to a little under 21,000, making PNC Park the fifth worst draw in the major leagues. If you're the type to go looking for scapegoats, don't blame the Pirates' little field—blame the players on it. The boys from Pittsburgh finished no better than thirteen games behind first place in the first three years in their new sandlot. With a performance like that, any stadium, even one as intimate and welcoming as PNC Park, stands a good chance of going empty on a regular basis.

BELOW: *The fans start to fill the stands at Cincinnati's Great American Ballpark before the opening game on March 31, 2003.* **OPPOSITE:** *Old-time Great American Ballpark, facing the Ohio River, is a well-deserved reward for all the years Reds fans endured the artificial turf at Riverfront Stadium.*

Great American Ball Park

Cincinnati
(opened 2003)

While Cincinnati's sparkling new ballpark lacks the charm of the new parks in San Francisco and Pittsburgh, this much is certain: it sure beats the dump it replaced. The Reds' old stadium, Cinergy Field (also known as "Riverfront Stadium" or "a big mistake," depending on whom you talk to) was universally loathed as a cold, impersonal concrete doughnut. After years of wrangling, the Reds' behemoth bit the dust and was replaced by cozy Great American Ball Park, named after the insurance company that paid up for the naming rights.

Cincinnati was so anxious for a new ballpark that they didn't even wait to rip down the old one before building the new one. In an interesting and unprecedented move, a "bite" was taken out of the outfield in old Cinergy Field in

January 2001 to make room for construction of Great American Ball Park. Just two years later, on March 31, 2003, former president George H.W. Bush threw out the first pitch, and a new era of Cincinnati baseball was born.

With a capacity of 42,059, Great American Ball Park holds more than 20 percent fewer fans than Cinergy Field and is drawing comparisons to Crosley Field, the beloved Reds ballpark that was bulldozed in 1972. Great American Ball Park sports an asymmetrical outfield and a Kentucky Bluegrass playing field, as well as many features that celebrate the history of the Reds. Along the back of the scoreboard, the signature sign-off of broadcaster Joe Nuxhall, "Rounding third and heading for home," greets the faithful, and an open outfield gives great views of the Ohio River. But contrary to many of the new-old revival parks, Great American Ball Park sports a more contemporary look, shedding the brick façade for a bright exterior. This stands

in sharp contrast to the bright red seats through-out the interior. One of the park's most peculiar features is a "notch" along the third base line between sections of the upper decks, with cat-walks in between offering a view of the visitor's bullpen below.

Great American Ball Park rates the same for attendance as it does on other scores, not stellar but a far cry better than its predecessor. In its final year of existence in 2002, Cinergy Field saw just over 23,000 fans per game, as compared to 29,077 per game in 2003 for the Reds' new ballpark, moving the Reds into the top 50 per-cent of clubs in attendance. In fact, Great American Ball Park saw the first sellout of a weekday afternoon game in more than four decades. Great American Ball Park may not be perfect, but it's a solid reward for fans of one of the oldest teams in Major League Baseball. Of course, with the Reds finishing nineteen games out of first place for the 2003 season, only time will tell if the novelty of a new ballpark can be sustained in the absence of a winning record for the home team.

ABOVE LEFT: *Good riddance: Cinergy Field in Cincinnati is imploded on December 29, 2002.*
ABOVE RIGHT: *The massive white steel infrastructure of Cincinnati's Great American Ball Park.*
LEFT: *The Reds battle the Pittsburgh Pirates on the opening day of their new ballpark, March 31, 2003.*

APPENDIX

Selected Statistics of Major League Ballparks

Note: All outfield dimensions given are current as of 2003; in the case of defunct parks, final dimensions are provided.

Arizona

Bank One Ballpark

Phoenix, AZ

401 E. Jefferson Street, PO Box 2095

Phoenix, AZ 85001

(602) 514-8500

Home Team: Arizona Diamondbacks

Opening Date: March 31, 1998

Capacity: 49,033

Outfield Dimensions: LF 328 feet
(100m); CF 402 feet (122.5m);
RF 335 feet (102.m)

Turf: Auza Grass (1998); Kentucky
Bluegrass (1999)

California

Edison International Field

Anaheim, CA

2000 Gene Autry Way

Anaheim, CA 92806

(888) 796-4256

Home Team: Anaheim Angels

Opening Date: April 19, 1966

Capacity (Original; Latest): 43,000;
45,050

Outfield Dimensions: LF 330 feet
(100.6m); CF 406 feet (123.7m);
RF 330 feet (100.6m)

Turf: Bluegrass

Dodger Stadium

Los Angeles, CA

1000 Elysian Park Avenue

Los Angeles, CA 90012

(323) 224-1400; Tickets (323) 224-1HIT

Home Team: Los Angeles Dodgers

Opening Date: April 10, 1962

Capacity: 56, 000

Outfield Dimensions: LF 330 feet
(100.6m); CF 395 feet (120.4m);
RF 330 feet (100.6m)

Turf: Santa Ana Bermuda Grass

**Network Associates Coliseum
(formerly Oakland-Alameda
County Coliseum)**

Oakland, CA

7000 Coliseum Way

Oakland, CA 94621

(510) 638-4900

Home Team: Oakland Athletics

Opening Date: April 17, 1968

Capacity (Original; Latest): 50,000;
48,219

Outfield Dimensions: LF 330 feet
(100.6m); CF 400 feet (121.9m);
RF 330 feet (100.6m)

Turf: Bluegrass

Qualcomm Stadium

San Diego, CA

9449 Friars Road

San Diego, CA 92108

(619) 452-SEAT

Home Team: San Diego Padres

Opening Date: August 20, 1967

Capacity (Original; Latest): 50, 000;
67,544

Outfield Dimensions: LF 327 feet
(99.7m); CF 405 feet (123.4m);
RF 330 feet (100.6m)

Turf: Santa Ana Bermuda Grass

**3Com Park
(formerly Candlestick Park)**

San Francisco, CA

Home Team: San Francisco Giants

Opening Date: April 12, 1960

Last Baseball Game: September 30, 1999

Capacity (Original; Last): 43,765;
58,000

Outfield Dimensions: LF 335 feet
(102.2m); CF 365 feet (111.3m);
RF 328 feet (99.9m)

Turf: Bluegrass (1960); Artificial (1971);
Bluegrass (1979)

SBC Park

San Francisco, CA

24 Willie Mays Plaza

San Francisco, CA 94107

(415) 972-2000

Home Team: San Francisco Giants

Opening Date: April 11, 2000

Capacity: 41,503

Outfield Dimensions: LF 335 feet
(102.1m); CF 404 feet (123.1m);
RF 307 feet (93.6m)

Turf: Grass

Colorado

Coors Field

Denver, CO

2001 Blake Street

Denver, CO 80205

(303) ROCKIES

Home Team: Colorado Rockies

Opening Date: April 26, 1995

Capacity (Original; Latest): 50,200;
50,381

Outfield Dimensions: LF 347 feet
(105.8m); CF 445 feet (135.6m);
RF 350 feet (106.7m)

Turf: Grass

Florida

**Pro Player Stadium
(formerly Joe Robbie Stadium)**

Miami, FL

2267 Dan Marino Boulevard

Miami, FL 33056

(305) 626-7400

Home Team: Florida Marlins

Opening Date: August 16, 1987; first
Marlins game: April 5, 1993

Capacity: 36,331

Outfield Dimensions: LF 330 feet
(100.6m); CF 434 feet (132.3m);
RF 345 feet (105.2m)

Turf: Tifway 419 Bermuda Grass

Tropicana Field

St. Petersburg, FL

1 Tropicana Drive

Petersburg, FL 33705

(888) 326-7297

Home Team: Tampa Bay Devil Rays

Opening Date: March 3, 1990; first Devil
Rays game: March 31, 1998

Capacity: 45,000

Outfield Dimensions: LF 315 feet
(96m); CF 404 feet (123.1m);
RF 322 feet (98.1m)

Turf: Astroturf with dirt infield

Georgia

Turner Field

Atlanta, GA

755 Hank Aaron Drive

Atlanta, GA 30302

(404) 522-7630

Home Team: Atlanta Braves

Opening Date: March 29, 1997

Capacity: 49,831

Outfield Dimensions: LF 335 feet
(102.1m); CF 401 feet (122.2m);
RF 330 feet (100.6m)

Turf: GN-1 Bermuda Grass

Illinois

Comiskey Park

Chicago, IL

Home Team: Chicago White Sox

Opening Date: July 1, 1910

Last Game: September 30, 1990

Capacity (Original; Last): 32,000;
52,000

Outfield Dimensions: LF 362 feet
(110.3m); CF 420 feet (128m);
RF 362 feet (110.3m)

Turf: Grass (1910); Artificial Infield
(1969); Grass Infield (1976)

**U.S. Cellular Field
(formerly New Comiskey Park)**

Chicago, IL

333 West 35th Street

Chicago, IL 60616

(312) 831-1SOX

Home Team: Chicago White Sox

Opening Date: April 18, 1991

Capacity: 47,098

Outfield Dimensions: LF 330 feet
(100.6m); CF 440 feet (134.1m);
RF 335 feet (102.1m)

Turf: Bluegrass

Wrigley Field

Chicago, IL

1060 West Addison Street

Chicago, IL 60613

(773) 404-CUBS

Home Team: Chicago Cubs

Opening Date: April 23, 1914

Capacity (Original; Latest): 14,000;
38,902

Outfield Dimensions: LF 355 feet
(108.2m); CF 400 feet (121.9m);
RF 353 feet (107.6m)

Turf: Merion Bluegrass and clover

Maryland

Oriole Park at Camden Yards

Baltimore, MD

333 West Camden Street

Baltimore, MD 21201

(401) 685-9800

Home Team: Baltimore Orioles

Opening Date: April 6, 1992

Capacity: 48,262

Outfield Dimensions: LF 333 feet
(101.5m); CF 400 feet (121.9m);
RF 318 feet (96.9m)

Turf: Maryland Bluegrass

Massachusetts

Fenway Park
Boston, MA
4 Yawkey Way
Boston, MA 02215-3496
(617) 267-1700
Home Team: Boston Red Sox
Opening Date: April 20, 1912
Capacity (Original; Latest): 58,000
    (1923); 33,993 (night), 33,577 (day)
Outfield Dimensions: LF 340 feet
    (94.5m); CF 420 feet (128m);
    RF 302 feet (92m)
Turf: Bluegrass

Michigan

Tiger Stadium
Detroit, MI
Home Team: Detroit Tigers
Opening Date: April 20, 1912
Last Game: September 27, 1999
Capacity (Original; Last): 23,000;
    52,416
Outfield Dimensions: LF 340 feet
    (103.6m); CF 440 feet (134.1m);
    RF 325 feet (99.1m)
Turf: Merion Bluegrass

Comerica Park
Detroit, MI
2100 Woodward
Detroit, MI 48201
(313) 471-2000
Home Team: Detroit Tigers
Opening Date: April 11, 2000
Capacity: 40,120
Outfield Dimensions: LF 345 feet
    (105.2m); CF 420 feet (128m);
    RF 330 feet (100.6m)
Turf: Grass

Minnesota

Hubert H. Humphrey Metrodome
Minneapolis, MN
34 Kirby Puckett Place
Minneapolis, MN 55415
(612) 375-1116 or (800) 33-TWINS
Home Team: Minnesota Twins
Opening Date: April 3, 1982
Capacity: 55,883
Outfield Dimensions: LF 344 feet
    (104.9m); CF 408 feet (124.4m);
    RF 327 feet (99.7m)
Turf: Astroturf

Missouri

Kauffman Stadium
Kansas City, MO
1 Royal Way
Kansas City, MO 64129
(816) 921-2200
Home Team: Kansas City Royals
Opening Date: April 10, 1973
Capacity: 40,625
Outfield Dimensions: LF 330 feet
    (100.6m); CF 400 feet (122m);
    RF 330 feet (100.6m)
Turf: Astroturf (1973); Grass (1995)

Busch Stadium
St. Louis, MO
250 Stadium Plaza
St. Louis, MO 63102
(314) 421-3060
Home Team: St. Louis Cardinals
Opening Date: May 12, 1966
Capacity: 49,676
Outfield Dimensions: LF 330 feet
    (100.6m); CF 402 feet (122.5m);
    RF 330 feet (100.6m)
Turf: Grass (1966); Artificial (1970);
    Grass (1996)

New York

Yankee Stadium
Bronx, NY
E. 161st Street
Bronx, NY 10451
(718) 293-6000
Home Team: New York Yankees
Opening Date: April 18, 1923
Capacity (Original; Latest): 58,000;
    57,545
Outfield Dimensions: LF 318 feet
    (96.9m); CF 408 feet (124.4m);
    RF 314 feet (95.7m)
Turf: Merion Bluegrass

Ebbets Field
Brooklyn, NY
Home Team: Brooklyn Dodgers
Opening Date: April 9, 1913
Last Game: September 24, 1957
Capacity (Original; Last): 25,000;
    32,000
Outfield Dimensions: LF 419 feet
    (106.1m); CF 450 feet (122m);
    RF 301 feet (107.6m)
Turf: Grass

Shea Stadium
Flushing, NY
123-01 Roosevelt Avenue
 Flushing, NY 11368
(718) 507-METS; Tickets (718) 507-TIXX
Home Team: New York Mets
Opening Date: April 17, 1964
Capacity: 55,601
Outfield Dimensions: LF 338 feet
    (103m); CF 410 feet (125m);
    RF 338 feet (103m)
Turf: Bluegrass

Polo Grounds (IV)

New York, NY

Home Teams: New York Giants
  1911–57; New York Yankees 1913–22;
  New York Mets 1962–63
Opening Date: June 28, 1911
Last Game: September 18, 1963
Capacity (Original; Last): 34,000;
  55,000
Outfield Dimensions: LF 279 feet
  (85m); CF 483 feet (147.2m);
  RF 257 feet (78.3m)
Turf: Grass

Ohio

Cinergy Field

Cincinnati, OH

Home Team: Cincinnati Reds
Opening Date: June 30, 1970
Last Game: September 22, 2002
Capacity: 52,952
Outfield Dimensions: LF 330 feet
  (100.6m); CF 404 feet (123.1m);
  RF 330 feet (100.6m)
Turf: Astroturf 8

Great American Ball Park

Cincinnati, OH

100 Main Street
Cincinnati, OH 45202
(513) 765-7000
Home Team: Cincinnati Reds
Opening Date: March 21, 2003
Capacity: 42,059
Outfield Dimensions: LF 328 feet
  (100m); CF 404 feet (123.1M);
  RF 325 feet (99m)
Turf: Grass

Jacobs Field

Cleveland, OH

2401 Ontario Street
Cleveland, OH 44115
(216) 420-4200
Home Team: Cleveland Indians
Opening Date: April 4, 1994
Capacity: 43,345
Outfield Dimensions: LF 325 feet
  (99.1m); CF 405 feet (123.4m);
  RF 325 feet (99.1m)
Turf: Kentucky Bluegrass

Ontario

SkyDome

Toronto, Ontario

One Blue Jays Way
Toronto, Ontario M5V 1J1
(416) 341-1234 or (888) 654-6528
Home Team: Toronto Blue Jays
Opening Date: June 5, 1989
Capacity: 50,516
Outfield Dimensions: LF 328 feet
  (100m); CF 400 feet (121.9m);
  RF 328 feet (99.9m)
Turf: Astroturf

Pennsylvania

Veterans Stadium

Philadelphia, PA

3501 South Broad Street
Philadelphia, PA 19148
(215) 463-1000
Home Team: Philadelphia Phillies
Opening Date: April 4, 1971
Last Game: September 28, 2003
Capacity: 62,382
Outfield Dimensions: LF 330 feet
  (100.6m); CF 408 feet (124.4m);
  RF 330 feet (100.6m)
Turf: Astroturf

Three Rivers Stadium

Pittsburgh, PA

600 Stadium Circle
Pittsburgh, PA 15212
(412) 321-2827 or (800) 289-2827
Home Team: Pittsburgh Pirates
Opening Date: July 16, 1970
Last Game: October 1, 2000
Capacity: 47,971
Outfield Dimensions: LF 335 feet
  (102.1m); CF 400 feet (121.9m);
  RF 335 feet (102.1m)
Turf: Tartanturf (1970); Astroturf (1983)

PNC Park

Pittsburgh, PA

115 Federal Street
Pittsburgh, PA 15212
(412) 323-5000
Home Team: Pittsburgh Pirates
Opening Date: March 31, 2001
Capacity: 38,365
Outfield Dimensions: LF 325 feet (99m);
CF 410 feet (125m); RF 320 feet (97.5)
Turf: Grass

Quebec

Olympic Stadium

Montreal, Quebec

4549 Pierre de Coubertin
Montreal, Quebec H1V 3N7
(514) 253-3434
Home Team: Montreal Expos
First Expos game: April 15, 1977
Capacity: 46,500
Outfield Dimensions: LF 325 feet
  (99.1m); CF 404 feet (123.1m);
  RF 325 feet (99.1m)
Turf: Astroturf

Texas

The Ballpark in Arlington

Arlington, TX

100 Ballpark Way

Arlington, TX 76011

(817) 273-5222; Tickets (817) 273-5000

Home Team: Texas Rangers

Opening Date: April 1, 1994

Capacity: 49,178

Outfield Dimensions: LF 334 feet
  (101.8m); CF 400 feet (121.9m);
  RF 325 feet (99.1m)

Turf: Tifway 419 Bermuda Grass

Astrodome

Houston, TX

Home Team: Houston Astros

Opening Date: April 12, 1965

Last Baseball Game: October 9, 1999

Capacity (Original; Last): 42,217
  (1965); 54,816 (1990)

Outfield Dimensions: LF 325 feet
  (99.1m); CF 400 feet (121.9m);
  RF 325 feet (99.1m)

Turf: Tifway 419 Bermuda Grass (1965);
  Astroturf (1966)

Minute Maid Park

Houston, TX

501 Crawford, Suite 400

Houston, TX 77002

(713) 259-8000

Home Team: Houston Astros

Opening Date: April 7, 2000

Capacity: 40,950

Outfield Dimensions: LF 315 feet (96m);
CF 435 feet (132.6m); RF 326 feet (99.4m)

Turf: Grass

Washington

SAFECO Field

Seattle, WA

83 King Street

Seattle, WA 98104

(206) 346-4000; Tickets (206) 622-HITS

Home Team: Seattle Mariners

Opening Date: July 15, 1999

Capacity: 47,116

Outfield Dimensions: LF 331 feet
  (100.9m); CF 405 feet (123.4m);
  RF 326 feet (99.4m)

Turf: Grass

Wisconsin

Milwaukee County Stadium

Milwaukee, WI

Home Team: Milwaukee Brewers

Opening Date: April 6, 1953

Last Game: September 28, 2000

Capacity (Original; Latest): 36,011;
  53,192

Outfield Dimensions: LF 315 feet
  (96m); CF 402 feet (122.5m);
  RF 315 feet (96m)

Turf: Bluegrass

Miller Park

Milwaukee, WI

One Brewers Way

Milwaukee, WI 53214

(414) 902-4400

Home Team: Milwaukee Brewers

Opening Date: April 6, 2001

Capacity: 42,400

Outfield Dimensions: LF 344 feet
  (104.9m); CF 400 feet (122m);
  RF 345 feet (105.2M)

Turf: Grass

SELECTED BIBLIOGRAPHY

Adams, Bruce, and Margaret Engel. *Ballpark Vacations: Great Family Trips to Minor League and Classic Major League Baseball Parks Across America.* New York: Fodor's Travel Publications, 1997.

Ahuja, Jay. *Fields of Dreams: A Guide to Visiting and Enjoying All 30 Major League Ballparks.* Secaucus, N.J.: Citadel Press, 1998.

Benson, Michael. *Ballparks of North America: A Comprehensive Historical Reference to Baseball Grounds, Yards and Stadiums, 1845 to Present.* Jefferson, N.C.: McFarland and Company, 1989.

Chadwick, Bruce, and David M. Spindel. *The Giants: Memories and Memorabilia from a Century of Baseball.* New York: Abbeville Press, 1993.

Gershman, Michael. *Diamonds: The Evolution of the Ballpark.* Boston: Houghton Mifflin Company, 1993.

Lowry, Philip J. *Green Cathedrals: The Ultimate Celebration of All 273 Major League and Negro League Ballparks Past and Present.* Reading, Mass.: Addison Wesley Publishing Co. 1992.

Palacios, Oscar, and Eric Robin. *Ballpark Sourcebook: Diamond Diagrams.* Skokie, Ill.: STATS Publishing, 1998.

Reidenbaugh, Lowell. *The Sporting News: Take Me Out to the Ballpark.* St. Louis: Sporting New Publishing Co., 1983.

Ritter, Lawrence S. *Lost Ballparks: A Celebration of Baseball's Legendary Fields.* New York: Penguin Studio Books, 1992.

Tackach, James, and Joshua B. Stein. *The Fields of Summer: America's Great Ballparks and the Players Who Triumphed in Them.* New York: Crescent Books, 1992.

Ward, Geoffrey C., and Ken Burns. *Baseball: An Illustrated History.* New York: Alfred A. Knopf, 1994.

Wood, Bob. *Dodger Dogs to Fenway Franks: The Ultimate Guide to America's Top Baseball Parks.* New York: McGraw Hill, 1988

The following websites were also consulted:

Ballparks by Munsey & Suppes (www.ballparks.com)

Ballpark Digest (www.ballparkwatch.com)

ESPN.com (sports.espn.go.com)

ABOVE: *The world-champion Philadelphia Athletics line up for a team photo, 1913.*

PAGE 138–139: *Fenway Park, whose outfield dimensions have changed over fifteen times since its opening in 1912, has the smallest foul territory in the majors.*

PHOTO CREDITS

©Russ Andorka: p. 112 left

AP/Wide World Photos: pp. 10–11, 34 bottom, 44–45

©Christopher Bain Collection: p. 78 top

Baseball Hall of Fame Library, Cooperstown, NY: p. 16 bottom, 26 top, 33 top, 38 left, 60, 65, 84 bottom inset, 89

©Jonathan Busser: p. 84

Corbis: p. 34 top, 41 middle, 54 bottom; AFP: p. 101 top, 107 inset; Bettmann: p. 8, 16 top, 24, 27 top, 29 bottom, 46 top, 47, 52, 62–63, 63 right,144; ©Mark E. Gibson: p. 79 top; ©Neal Preston: p. 64; ©Reuters NewMedia Inc.: p. 74 top, 120 top, 123; ©Schenectady Museum; Hall of Electrical History Foundation: p. 76 inset; ©Ted Streshinsky: p. 61; UPI: p. 30 top, 46 bottom, 53 bottom

©David Durochik: p. 119 top

eStock Photography: ©Thomason Productions: p. 69

Everlasting Images, Inc.: "The Rob Arra Collection/ www.EverlastingImages.com: pp. 42–43, 50–51, 66–67, 90–91 bottom, 96–97 bottom, 100–101 bottom, 108–109 bottom, 114–115 bottom, 118–119 bottom, 120–121 bottom, 124–125, 126–127 bottom, 130–131 bottom, 138–139

Getty Images: AllSport USA: ©Tom Brokema: p. 48; ©Jonathan Daniel: p. 21 bottom, 29 top, 49, 122 bottom, 128, 129, 131; ©Stephen Dunn: pp. 20–21, 99, 100 top, 108 top; ©Otto Greule, Jr.: pp. 110–111; ©Tom Hauck: p. 17, 116–117; ©Jeff Hixon: p. 73 bottom, 79 bottom; ©Vincent LaForet: pp. 22–23; ©Zoran Milich: pp. 56, 58; ©Don Smith: pp. 18–19; ©Jamie Squire: p. 127 top; ©Rick Stewart: pp. 59, 95 bottom; ©Matthew Stockman: pp. 70–71; FPG International: pp. 6–7, 53 top; ©James Blank: p. 75; ©Jerry Driendl: p. 81; ©Peter Gridley, p. 14–15; ©Michael Hart, p. 68; ©Jay Lurie, p. 77; ©Gary Randall,

94–95; ©Michael Tamborrino: p. 55 inset; ©Paul S. Howell: p. 115 top; ©Allan Kee: p. 98; ©Ronald Martinez: pp. 112–113; ©Mike Simmons: p. 130 top

©Index Stock: pp. 82–83

Library of Congress: p. 12 bottom, 13, 26–27 bottom, 32–33 bottom, 34 top, 36 middle inset, 36–37 bottom, 37 inset, 40–41 bottom, 76, 80 bottom, 137, 140, 142–143

MBR Images: pp. 92–93, 102–103

New England Stock Photo: ©Thomas H. Mitchell: p. 43 right; ©Jim Schwabel: p. 73 top

©Kathryn Siegler: p. 1, 117 right

©David Spindel: p. 10, 30 center, 32 middle, 36 top inset, 40 inset, 41 top, 43 right, 47 insets, 54 top, 60 inset, 67 bottom, 69 inset, 72, 74 bottom, 77 top, 78 bottom, 82 inset, 92 top and bottom, 95 top, 102 inset, 122 top

Sports Chrome, Inc.: ©Rob Tringali: pp. 2–3, 55, 97 top; ©Scott Troyanos: p. 106, 107

Sports Imagery: p. 35; ©Gene Boyars: pp. 28–29, 38–39

©Tim Jackson: p. 86, 104–105

Transparencies, Inc.: ©Peter Zay: p. 85

Unicorn Stock Photos: ©ChromaSohn: p. 31

Woodfin Camp & Associates: ©Bernard Boutrit: p. 21 top

BELOW: *Fans line up on the sidelines at the final game of the 1905 World Series. After the New York Giants defeated the Philadelphia Athletics the crowd rushed the field, and the victorious Giants had to take refuge in their clubhouse until the police could restore order.*

INDEX

A

Aaron, Hank, 61
Air conditioning, 106
Allen, Dick, 68
American League, 26, 36, 37, 96
Anaheim Angels, 17
Anderson, Dave, 61
Anderson, Sparky, 37
Appling, Luke, 29
Arizona Diamondbacks, 107
Arlington Stadium, 99
Artificial turf, 58, 61, 68, 69, 69, 74, 77, 78, 84, 89
Astrodome (Houston), 58, 68, 68, 69, 69, 70–71, 112
Astros Field (Houston), 114
Atlanta Braves, 122
Atlanta-Fulton County Stadium (Atlanta), 89, 89

B

Ballpark at Union Station (Houston), 112
Ballpark in Arlington, 36, 99, 99, 100, 101, 101
Ballparks
  beginning of permanent structures, 26
  brick, 26, 45, 99, 102, 106, 118, 126
  capacity, 16
  classic era, 25–55
  concrete donut style, 16, 72–81
  cookie-cutter, 72
  double decked, 30, 32, 45, 78, 126
  double-decked, 29
  field sizes, 12, 13, 37, 41, 45, 46, 53, 54, 91, 95, 121, 128
  lighting, 48
  modern era, 57–86
  multipurpose, 68, 72, 106, 120, 126
  natural capacity of, 27
  revival era, 87–131
  shared with football teams, 16, 61
  single decked, 29
  steel/concrete, 16, 26, 32, 58
  triple decked, 54, 74, 77
  wildcat bleachers, 27, 36
  wooden, 32
Baltimore Orioles, 77
Bank One Ballpark (Phoenix), 106, 106, 107, 107
Banks, Ernie, 92
Barber, Red, 45
Belli, Melvin, 61
Bennett Park (Detroit), 36
Big O. See Olympic Stadium
Big Red Machine. See Cincinnati Reds
Black Sox scandal, 29–30
Blood Angle (Yankee Stadium), 54
BOB. See Bank One Ballpark
Bolles, John, 61
Bonds, Barry, 117, 118, 119
Boston Braves, 40
Boston Red Sox, 29, 53
Boyer, Clete, 30
Briggs, Walter, 36
Briggs Stadium (Detroit), 36
Brooklyn Dodgers, 64
Brotherhood Park (New York), 32
Brush Stadium (New York), 32
Burns, Ken, 46
Busch Stadium (St.Louis), 72, 72, 74, 75, 75
Bush, George H.W., 128

C

Camden Yards (Baltimore), 14–15, 27, 45, 90, 90, 91, 91, 92, 93, 102, 118
Candlestick Park (San Francisco), 16, 58, 60, 61, 62, 63, 63, 74, 117
Capacity
  Briggs Stadium, 36–37
  Busch Stadium, 75
  Candlestick Park, 61
  Comerica Park, 121
  Comiskey Park, 29
  Crosley Field, 76
  Dodger Stadium, 66
  Ebbets Field, 46
  Fenway Park, 43
  Jacobs Field, 95
Jarry Park, 83
Minute Maid Park, 114
Olympic Stadium, 85
PNC Park, 78, 126
Polo Grounds, 32
Riverfront Stadium. See Cincinnati Reds
SAFECO Field, 108
Shibe Park, 26
Three Rivers Stadium, 78
Tiger Stadium, 38
Cartwright, Alexander, 25
Cey, Ron, 64, 64
Chicago Cubs, 29, 48, 49
Chicago Whales, 48
Chicago White Sox, 28, 29, 30
Cincinnati Reds, 76, 77, 128, 129, 131
Cinergy Field (Cincinnati), 13, 76, 77, 77, 129, 130
Citizens Bank Park (Philadelphia), 81
Clemente, Roberto, 48, 126
Cleveland Stadium, 95
Cobb, Ty, 36, 36
Cochrane Plan, 38
The Coliseum (Oakland), 18–19
Colorado Rockies, 102, 105
Comerica Park (Detroit), 38, 96, 120, 120–121
Comiskey, Charles, 28
Comiskey Park (Chicago), 28, 28, 29, 29, 30, 30, 31, 90, 96
Connie Mack Stadium (Philadelphia), 80
Coogan's Bluff, 16, 32
Coors Field (Denver), 22, 86, 87, 96, 102, 103, 104, 105
County Stadium (Milwaukee), 78, 122, 126
Cricket, 25
Crosley Field (Cincinnati), 13, 58, 76, 76, 77, 128

D

Davis, Zachary Taylor, 28
Dawson, Andre, 85
Day, John, 32
Death Valley (Yankee Stadium), 54
Denver Pacific Depot, 102
Designated hitter, 27
Detroit Tigers, 9, 30, 120, 121
DiMaggio, Joe, 54
Dodger Stadium (Los Angeles), 16, 58, 63, 64, 65, 66, 66, 67, 67, 118
Dombrowski, Dave, 121
Dotel, Octavio, 114, 114
Dykes, Jimmy, 30

E

Ebbet, Charles, 45, 46
Ebbets Field (Brooklyn), 13, 26, 27, 44, 45, 46, 46, 47, 58, 96, 118
Edison Field (Anaheim), 17, 17
Elysian Fields (Hoboken), 26, 26
Enron Field (Houston), 112
Expansion teams, 13, 68, 83

F

Federal League, 48
Fenway Park (Boston), 40, 40, 41, 41, 42
Florida Marlins, 58
Forbes Field (Pittsburgh), 13, 58, 78, 78

G

Garner, Phil, 61
Gehrig, Lou, 54, 92
Gershman, Michael, 36, 37, 68
Gibson, Kirk, 37
Great American Ball Park (Cincinnati), 77, 128, 128, 129, 129, 130, 131
Green Monster, 41, 43, 43
Groundskeeping, 30, 48, 66, 89, 109

H

Hebner, Richie, 72
Henry, John, 43
Hofheinz, Roy, 68
"The House That Ruth Built." See Yankee Stadium
Houston Astros, 112

Houston Colt .45s, 68
Huggins, Miller, 54

I

In play ladder, 41, 43, *43*

J

Jackson, Reggie, 54
Jackson, "Shoeless" Joe, 29,
    29, 30
Jackson, Sonny, 119
Jacobs, Eli, 90
Jacobs, Richard, 38, 96
Jacobs Field (Cleveland), 22,
    27, 88, *88*, 89, *94*, 95,
    95–*96*, 96, 97, 118
Jarry Park (Montreal), 83
Johnson, Randy, 107

K

Kansas City Royals, 21
Kauffman Stadium (Kansas
    City), *20*, 21
Kingdome (Seattle), 89, 108,
    108, 109
Kluszewski, Ted, 74
Knickerbocker Base Ball Club,
    25, 26

L

Landis, Kennisaw Mountain,
    30, *30*
Lane, Frank, 30
Lane Rule, 30
Larsen, Don, 54

Legends of the Game Baseball
    Museum (Arlington), 99
Lemon, Jim, 41
Loria, Jeffrey, 85
Los Angeles Dodgers, 45, 57,
    118
Luzinski, Greg, 80

M

Magowan, Peter, 117
Mantle, Mickey, 54
Maris, Roger, 54, 74
Martinez, Pedro, 85
Mays, Willie, 33, 61, *61*, 118
McCovey, Willie, 118
McCovey Cove (SBC Park),
    117, 118
McGraw, John, 33, 53
McGwire, Mark, 74, *74*
McLane, Drayton, 68, 112
Memorial Park (Yankee
    Stadium), 55, *55*
Memorial Stadium
    (Baltimore), 90
Metrodome (Minneapolis), 21,
    21, 22
Metropolitans, 32
Miller, Stu, 61
Miller Park (Milwaukee), 122,
    123, *123*, *124–125*
Milwaukee Braves, 122
Milwaukee Brewers, 122
Minnesota Twins, 22, 121
Minute Maid Park (Houston),
    68, 112, *113*, 114, *114*,
    115, 116

Moehler, Brian, 120
Monroe, Lucy, 46
Montreal Expos, 83, 85
Murdoch, Rupert, 67
Murray, Eddie, 92

N

National League, 26, 32, 46,
    83, 119
National Register of Historic
    Places, 37
Navin, Frank, 36
Navin Field, 37, *37*
Neel, Eric, 126
New York Giants, 12, 29, 32,
    35, 53
New York Knickerbockers,
    25, 26
New York Mets, 12, 13, 32,
    35, 121
New York Nine, 26
New York Yankees, 12, 30, 32,
    33
Nicholson, Bill, 48
Nixon, Richard, 61
Nuxhall, Joe, 128

O

Oakland Athletics, 61
Olympic Stadium (Montreal),
    82, 83, 84, *84*, 85, *85*
O'Malley, Walter, 46, 64, 66
Oriole Park at Camden Yards.
    See Camden Yards
    (Baltimore)

P

Pacific Bell Park (San
    Francisco), 45, 89, 119, *119*
Palace of The Fans
    (Cincinnati), 76
Penn, Howard, 105
Perry, Gaylord, 61
Philadelphia Athletics, 32, 40,
    80
Philadelphia Phillies, 80, 81
Pittsburgh Buccaneers, 78
Pittsburgh Pirates, 35, 61, 78,
    131
Players League, 32
PNC Park (Pittsburgh), 78,
    126, *126*, 127, *127*
Polo Grounds (New York), 12,
    12, 13, *13*, 16, *16*, 26, 32,
    32, 33, *33*, 34, *34*, 35, *35*,
    53, 58
Pro Player Stadium (Miami),
    58, *58*

Q

Qualcomm Stadium (San
    Diego), 22, *23*

R

Reinsdorf, Jerry, 30
Ripkin, Cal Jr., 90, *90*, 91–92
Ritter, Lawrence, 29, 45
Riverfront Stadium
    (Cincinnati), 76, 77, 128
Robinson, Jackie, 46, *47*, 84
Rodriguez, Henry, 85
Rodriguez, Ivan, 101, *101*

Roofs, retractable, 83, 84, 85,
    85, 106, 107, *107*, 108,
    110–111, 114, *115, 122*
Ruth, Babe, 29, 30, 33, 40, *41*,
    48, 53, *53*, 54, *54*, 92
Ryan, Mike, 80

S
SAFECO Field (Seattle), 89,
    96, 108, 109, *109,
    110–111*
St. Louis Browns, 74
St. Louis Cardinals, 61, 74, 75
San Diego Padres, 37
San Francisco Giants, 13, 35,
    58, 61, 76, 117, 118, 119
SBC Park (San Francisco), 22,
    63, 96, 117, *117*, 118, *118*,
    119, *119*
Schaefer, William Donald, 90
Schmidt, Mike, 81
Scoreboards
    digital, 91
    exploding, 30, 48
    manual, 48, 74, 102
Seattle Mariners, 31, 89, 108
Seattle Pilots, 122
Shea Stadium (New York), 13,
    35, *35*, 54
Sherman, Ed, 95
Shibe Park (Philadelphia), 13,
    16, *16*, 26, *26, 27*, 80, *80*
Simmons, Al, 30
Sky Boxes (Astrodome), 68
SkyDome (Toronto), *56*, 58, *59*
Snider, Duke, *44*, 45, 46, *46*

Sosa, Sammy, 48, *48*
Sousa, John Philip, 54
South Side Park (Chicago), 28
Sparks, Steve, 121
Sportsman's Park (St.Louis),
    74, *74*
Stargell, Willie, 61
Staub, Rusty, 85
Steinbrenner, George, 54
Stengel, Casey, 30, 54
Stoneham, Horace, 35, 61
Sun Pool Party Pavilion (Bank
    One Ballpark), 106

T
Texas Rangers, 36, 99
3Com Park (San Francisco), 16
Three Rivers Stadium
    (Pittsburgh), 13, 16, 72,
    73, 78, *79*, 126
Ticket prices, 12
Tiger Stadium (Detroit), 37,
    37, 38, *38*, 39, *39*, 90
Tiger Stadium Fan Club, 37,
    38
Turner Field (Atlanta), 89, *89*
Turnpike Stadium (Arlington),
    99

U
Uecker, Bob, 123
U.S. Cellular Field (Chicago),
    28, 31, *31*

V
Vanderbeck, George, 36

Veeck, Bill, 30, 48
Veterans Stadium
    (Philadelphia), 16, 72, *73*,
    80, 81, *81*

W
Walk of Fame (Ballpark at
    Arlington), 99
Wallach, Tim, 85
Walsh, Ed, 28–29
Ward, Geoffrey, 46
Washburn, Ray, 61
Weeghman, Charlie, 48
Weeghman Park (Chicago), 48
Wertz, Vic, 33
Western League, 36
Wildcat bleachers, 27
Williams, Ted, 40, 41
Willie Mays Plaza (SBC Park),
    118
Wood, Bob, 80
World Series
    1905, 16
    1907, 36
    1908, 36, 49
    1909, 36
    1911, 32
    1912, 32
    1914, 40
    1917, 29
    1918, 29
    1919, 29
    1932, 48
    1935, 36
    1941, 54
    1945, 9, 37

    1956, 54
    1957, 122
    1963, 66
    1968, 37
    1970, 77
    1978, 64
    1980, 80
    1984, 37
    1989, 61, 63
    1995, 96
    1997, 96
    2002, 119
Wrigley, William Jr., 48
Wrigley Field (Chicago), 8, 9,
    12, 27, 28, 48, 49, *49*,
    50–51, 96

Y
Yankee Stadium (New York),
    10–11, 12, 21, *21*, 26, *52*,
    53, *53*, 55, *55*, 109
Yastrzemski, Carl, 41

The Chicago Cubs and the Pittsburgh Pirates face off in Pittsburgh on July 2, 1908.

*With the exodus of the Giants
to San Francisco, and the
Mets moving to the newly-
built Shea Stadium, the Polo
Grounds met the wrecking
ball in 1964.*

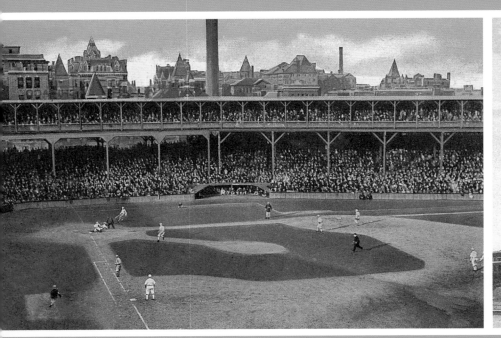